READING
William S. Gray

A RESEARCH RETROSPECTIVE, 1881-1941
John T. Guthrie, Editor

Reprinted by the
INTERNATIONAL READING ASSOCIATION, INC.
800 Barksdale Road, Box 8139, Newark, Delaware 19714

INTERNATIONAL READING ASSOCIATION

OFFICERS
1983-1984

President Ira E. Aaron, University of Georgia, Athens

Vice President Bernice E. Cullinan, New York University, New York City

Vice President Elect John C. Manning, University of Minnesota, Minneapolis

Executive Director Ralph C. Staiger, International Reading Association, Newark, Delaware

DIRECTORS

Term Expiring Spring 1984
Phylliss Adams, University of Denver, Colorado
John Downing, University of Victoria, British Columbia, Canada
Sara Scroggins, St. Louis Public Schools, Missouri

Term Expiring Spring 1985
Bobbye S. Goldstein, New York City Public Schools, New York
Doris Roettger, Heartland Education Agency, Ankeny, Iowa
Judith N. Thelen, Frostburg State College, Frostburg, Maryland

Term Expiring Spring 1986
Marie M. Clay, University of Auckland, Auckland, New Zealand
Dale D. Johnson, University of Wisconsin, Madison
Barbara M. Valdez, North Sacramento School District, Sacramento, California

Copyright 1984 by the
International Reading Association, Inc.

Library of Congress Cataloging in Publication Data

Gray, William S. (William Scott), 1885-1960.
   Reading : A research retrospective, 1881-1941.

   Reprinted from: Encyclopedia of educational research.
New York : Macmillan, 1941.
   Bibliography: p.
   Includes index.
   1. Reading—Research—Evaluation. I. Guthrie,
John T. II. Title.
LB1050.2.G72   1984   428.4'072   83-26677
ISBN 0-87207-959-7

CONTENTS

Preface   *John T. Guthrie*   v
Foreword   *Jeanne S. Chall*   viii

READING*   *William S. Gray*   1
   I. Sociology of Reading   7
  II. Nature of Reading and Basic Processes Involved   17
 III. Factors Related to Growth in Reading   31
 IV. Interest in Reading   40
  V. Reading Readiness   48
 VI. Aims, Organization, and Time Allotment of Reading in the Grades   54
VII. Nature, Content, and Grade Placement of Reading Materials   59
VIII. Methods of Teaching   64
 IX. Reading in the Content Fields   73
  X. Diagnosis and Remedial Teaching   78
 XI. Hygiene of Reading   83

*Reprinted from *Encyclopedia of Educational Research*, Walter S. Monroe, Editor. Prepared under the auspices of The American Educational Research Association, published by The Macmillan Company. Copyright 1941 by American Educational Research Association. Reprinted by permission.

IRA PUBLICATIONS COMMITTEE 1983-1984 Joan Nelson-Herber, State University of New York at Binghamton, *Chair* • Phylliss J. Adams, University of Denver • Janet R. Binkley, IRA • Nancy Naumann Boyles, North Haven, Connecticut, Board of Education • Faye R. Branca, IRA • Martha Collins-Cheek, Louisiana State University • Alan Crawford, California State University at Los Angeles • Susan Mandel Glazer, Rider College • Jerome C. Harste, Indiana University • Nelly M. Hecker, Furman University • Roselmina Indrisano, Boston University • Douglas Inkpen, G.B. Little Public School, Scarborough, Ontario • Eleanor Ladd, University of South Carolina • James R. Layton, Southwest Missouri State University • Irving P. McPhail, Johns Hopkins University • Caroline Neal, West Virginia College of Graduate Studies • P. David Pearson, University of Illinois • María Elena Rodríguez, Asociación Internacional de Lectura, Buenos Aires • Betty D. Roe, Tennessee Technological University • S. Jay Samuels, University of Minnesota • Ralph C. Staiger, IRA • Sam Weintraub, State University of New York at Buffalo.

The International Reading Association attempts, through its publications, to provide a forum for a wide spectrum of opinions on reading. This policy permits divergent viewpoints without assuming the endorsement of the Association.

Preface

John T. Guthrie
International Reading Association

William S. Gray was the preeminent reading educator. According to Arthur Gates, "Dr. Gray labored to improve the teaching of reading for a longer period of time (more than half a century), with greater singleness of purpose and in a wider variety of enterprises than anyone else in history."

William Scott Gray was born on June 5, 1885. As a young man of 19, he taught two years in the schools of rural Illinois. Recognized as a leader, he was promoted to Principal of elementary schools in Fowler, Illinois, where he served for three years. He continued his education at Illinois State Normal University, graduating with a teaching certificate in 1910. In the following two years he was Principal of the training school at Illinois State Normal, during which time he studied at the University of Chicago, receiving the Bachelor's degree in 1913.

Seeking the highest order of intellectual stimulation, Gray moved to Teachers College, Columbia University. Gray's interest in measurement, which formed the foundation of his first research and eventually led to the Gray Oral Reading Test, was nurtured by Edward Thorndike who was a leader of the mental testing movement. However, Gray placed a premium on educational studies per se and moved back to Chicago with a Master's degree in 1914. An avid student, he received the Ph.D. in 1916 from the Department of Education at the University of Chicago.

Gray continued his distinguished teaching career at the University of Chicago in 1914, with the position of Assistant in Education. Promotions were granted to him almost annually. Gray became an Instructor in 1915; he was given a faculty position as Assistant Professor in 1917. Later in the same year, he accepted the appointment of Dean of the College of Education, a position which he retained until 1931. In the following year he was elevated to Associate Professor and from 1921 to 1950, he committed himself unrelentingly to a Professorship.

His formal scholarship was launched with the publication of his dissertation by the University of Chicago Press in 1917, entitled *Studies of Elementary School Reading through Standardized Tests*. Gray conducted empirical studies throughout his lifetime. These are exemplified in such works as *Reading Interests and Habits of Adults*, which was a series of reading surveys conducted with the assistance of a librarian, Ruth Monroe, and published in 1929. He examined the purposes for reading and diversity of topics to which people are attracted, reported in *Maturity in Reading*, written with Bernice Rogers and published in 1956. Among many other practical titles, he published *Classroom Techniques on Improving Reading* in 1949, which signaled his continuous devotion to the needs of teachers for the fresh insights and renewed enthusiasm that may be derived from exposure to recent research.

During his active career as a Professor, Gray published 407 books, book chapters, and articles. Retiring in 1950, Gray saw the opportunity for heightened productivity. In the following 10 years as he moved from 65 to 75 years of age, he published 100 books, chapters, and articles for research journals. It required a bizarre accident, a fatal fall from a horse during a vacation with his wife, to end his prodigious career.

Gray's leadership was professional as well as intellectual. He chaired yearbook committees for the National Society for the Study of Education in 1924, 1936, and 1948. These efforts were consummated by recommendations for reform in reading programs from kindergarten through the college levels. Professional societies did not escape his attention. He was President of the American Educational Research Association in 1932-1933.

The International Reading Association elected him as its first President in 1956, which was a tribute both to the man and the Association.

Gray anticipated the trend for research synthesis as a basis of reasoned generalizations. He published summaries of research in the *Journal of Educational Research*, but also in other locations. Drawn from the *Encyclopedia of Educational Research*, edited by Walter Monroe in 1941, one of his remarkable manuscripts is reproduced here. The themes to which he points are based on more than 2,000 inquiries on reading from the dawn of literacy to 1941. Eminently qualified as a review of reviews, this monograph warrants acknowledgment in any scholarship on reading which claims the name of originality.

I am grateful to Jeanne Chall for drawing attention to the timeliness of Gray's review in the Foreword. Her observations are particularly apt, since she authored the entry on "Reading" in the fifth edition of the *Encyclopedia of Educational Research* in 1982.

Foreword

Jeanne S. Chall
Harvard University

The monograph by William S. Gray was initially published as the article, "Reading," in the first edition of the *Encyclopedia of Educational Research* in 1941. It contains a review of research on reading, with its implications for practice and for society. Gray went further, reviewing the scientific research trends from their beginnings in the late 1800s to the late 1930s, the date of his writing.

The review is remarkable from several viewpoints. First, it is extremely comprehensive, covering research on many topics that have long been familiar to us—from the sociology of reading to the nature of reading; from basic processes to diagnosis and remedial teaching. Certainly other historians of reading research may point to investigations not included by Gray. However, his treatment contains such topics as reading in the content areas, the hygiene of reading, and the aims, organizations, and time allotment of reading in the different grades.

Gray's treatment is remarkable for its broad historical sweep of the scientific study of reading and for its optimism about the power of reading research to improve instruction. Although Gray continually refers with enthusiasm to the growth of the research and to its constructive contributions toward understanding the reading process, he was not without criticism of the research and its applications.

The following excerpt speaks to both the criticism and the praise:

> But the progress achieved thus far is not without serious limitations. Unfortunately much of the scientific work relating to reading has been

fragmentary in character....the investigator frequently attacks an isolated problem, completes his study of it, and suggests that he will continue his research at some later time but often fails to do so. In the second place, there is little or no coordination of effort among research workers in the field of reading. In the third place, many of the studies reported have been conducted without adequate controls.... Nevertheless, much of the evidence available is so significant that it serves as a valuable guide in reorganizing and improving instruction in reading at all levels and in defining with greater clarity the function of reading in contemporary life. (pp. 892-893)

Thus, although Gray saw problems, he also saw progress. He expressed his deep faith and commitment to the objective study of reading that would ultimately lead to a better guide for reorganizing and improving instruction. For Gray, it seems that research and instruction were one, and that the health of one would be tied to the health of the other.

Gray's monograph is noteworthy for its meticulous reporting of relevant reading studies, of their contributions to practice, and of the trends from preceding periods in relation to the one in which he wrote. Thus, we learn that the period of 1911 to 1920 marked the beginning of broader interest in the scientific study of reading, and clearer recognition of the need to apply objective methods to classroom problems. In this time, a variety of studies

...related to such issues as methods of learning to read, the relative merits of different methods of beginning reading, the value of phonics, the content of courses of study in reading, and the amount and quality of reading material in various schools and grades. (p. 892)

Gray discussed this trend by comparing it to studies made in the preceding periods.

To what extent were these attitudes toward reading research uniquely characteristic of W.S. Gray? Or were they characteristic of investigators of that time? And if a style of the time or Gray's alone, how do they relate to the style of today?

It is difficult to separate the style of a person from that of his time, especially when the person was the first of his time—as investigator, teacher educator, and curriculum developer. As a leader in the educational research on reading, Gray wrote for many years the annual reviews of reading research (now published annually by IRA), trained teachers and reading specialists, and authored the most widely used basal reading series. To be accepted as the leader by so many meant that his style was widely valued.

How does this enthusiasm for objective studies and optimism about the value of research for practice compare with the prevailing style today? How concerned are we now about the historical trends in our field and about carefully analyzing and interpreting research with regard to practice?

These are difficult questions and I raise them more for "thinking about" than for answering. But I suggest that some of the questions may receive some consensus, if they are raised.

Interest in history and historical trends in research does not seem to be as common among researchers today as it was in the early 1940s. Since research has burgeoned in the past 40 years, it is difficult enough to review the relatively recent research on any topic, much less return to earlier periods. Other factors are no doubt involved. One may be that computerized literature banks go back only to 1965, and the knowledge and tools needed for making a non-computerized search of earlier studies may not exist as widely as needed. Also, there seem to be common misconceptions among some researchers that only the research of the last 5, or at most 10 years, needs to be searched and read.

A reading of Gray's monograph may make some of us aware of a change. Today we seldom see Gray's warm enthusiasm for the value of scientific studies of reading. We rarely encounter his optimism about the uses of research for the improvement of reading instruction at all ages and for social policy with regard to literacy. Instead, the field is inclined toward clusters of enthusiasm for one or another special theory, for special basic and applied research, and for leaving to still others the application of the research to instruction.

Why the change? It no doubt comes from the great increase in reading research. It could also be related to the variety of researchers entering the field from such disciplines as linguistics, psycholinguistics, neurology, psychoneurology, cognitive psychology, computer sciences, educational psychology, special education, language development, human development, and the like. Indeed, Gray expressed such concern in 1941, noting an increase in specialization and fragmentation, with the blessings and problems they bring.

Much of the style of reading research seems to have changed during the past decades, particularly with regard to its applications to educational practice. Yet the topics and questions researched, the basic methodologies used, and the research findings summarized by Gray in 1941 seem surprisingly familiar when compared to the research of the past decade. There are so many examples of similarity that I can cite only a few.

A recent trend among some reading researchers is to relate teachers' concepts of reading to their different methods of teaching. One may become a bit humbled by Gray's discussion of the "three concepts" of reading based on the nature of reading as described by different investigators. According to Gray, one concept of reading emphasizes word recognition, one emphasizes meaning, and one is concerned with the significance of the meanings (p. 897).

Gray's monograph contains a section on reading comprehension that foretells present theory and research. The following sentence, in fact, portends present-day schema theory: "Only in so far as the reader's experiences relate in some form or other to the concepts or situations to which the author refers can the reader comprehend what is read" (p. 901).

Gray's reference to the importance of vocabulary in reading comprehension also forecasts current theory and research. "It follows that a readers' meaning vocabulary in terms of extent and richness is of large importance. In fact, it correlates more highly with comprehension than any other factor studied thus far except intelligence" (p. 901). One can find such statements, with almost the same freshness and sense of discovery, in a recent volume on basic and applied research on reading comprehension.*

Gray presents exciting generalizations from the research he reviewed on reading readiness, speed of reading, the relation of oral to silent reading, the effect of content and style on reading speed, the factors in word meaning development, how best to teach word meanings, and the like. Even such relatively current

---

*Guthrie, John T. (Ed.). *Comprehension and teaching: Research reviews.* See especially chapter on "Vocabulary knowledge" by Anderson & Freebody.

areas of study as reading stages, time on task, and direct versus less structured instruction are discussed. The uses of teaching tools, such as the typewriter, and the importance of practice in reading in the different content areas are not neglected.

Gray makes some very important points on research in readability that are being made today by cognitively oriented reading researchers. When he wrote in the late 1930s, most of the widely used readability formulas had not yet been developed. Yet he anticipated that future study of readability would include the challenging problem of studying readability in relation to the nature of the concepts included in the text.

This superb review is sobering. Have we perhaps tended to pay too little attention to the research richness of our past? Do we do so in our eagerness to make our own discoveries? If so, what do we gain by studying anew the questions and concepts that have been studied in the past? Are we aware of what has already been learned?

Gray opted for using the knowledge of the past to understand the present and future. Would he tell us to do the same today, even with the phenomenal increase in research? My guess is that he would. His monograph is testimony that the reading research of the past can bring benefits both to research and to practical uses of it.

READING
William S. Gray

The reading of written and printed symbols had its origin in the remote past when man first began to use pictures and other characters to send messages and to record events. The art of interpreting these characters and of teaching others to do so developed concurrently. The transition from picture writing to the use of letters representing specific sounds came very slowly and as a result of great effort. As early as twenty-five centuries before Christ, however, the Egyptians had analyzed words and syllables into sounds and had developed a series of symbols to represent them. Through the ingenuity of the Semites (24: 36-37) these sounds and symbols gave rise to the Phoenician alphabet from which developed in turn the Greek letters and the Roman alphabet.

As the arts of writing and reading improved, it is natural that they should acquire a significant place in the education of the more advanced nations. In the case of Greece reading was a subject of great importance long before the Battle of Marathon (490 B.C.). The procedure in learning to read was to master the letters, then the syllables, and finally the words. Throughout the centuries that followed, problems relating to reading provoked constant thought and discussion. As indicated by the studies of Lamport (31), the problems attacked most vigorously in the past related largely to methods of teaching beginning reading. In securing needed information and in reaching decisions, observations and personal judgments were relied on chiefly. Very little evidence of the use of scientific methods in studying reading problems appears in the literature until about the middle of the nineteenth century. Consequently, all the data presented in subsequent sections of this report were secured within the past century, and most of them since the beginning of the current century.

Development of Interest in the Scientific Study of Reading

Scientific studies relating to reading had their origin in the laboratories of Europe as a result of the curiosity of psychologists concerning the nature of the reading act and the way in which words are recognized. As early as 1844 Valentius became keenly interested in the nature of the perceptual processes in reading. His studies were followed in the course of time by those of Cattell, Erdmann, Dodge, and others, the results of which supported the conclusion (1: 3) that we read by phrases, words, or letters, according to the reader's familiarity with the reading matter and the difficulties which he encounters. A second series of studies grew out of interest in the behavior of the eyes in reading. About 1879 Javal made the important discovery that eye movements in reading are discontinuous, consisting of a series of alternate movements and pauses. This discovery was very illuminating and led to numerous studies during the next three decades concerning such problems as the nature, function, and relation of fixation movements and pauses, the possibility of vision during fixation movements, and the location and length of fixation pauses.

The early studies of perception and eye movements proved to be highly significant (1: 4). First, the facts secured presented a new and stimulating view of the nature of reading and of some of the processes involved. Second, the findings suggested many new problems for investigation and stimulated deeper interest in the scientific study of reading. Third, rapid progress was made in the development of experimental techniques and mechanical devices with which to secure accurate, objective records. A broad foundation was thus laid for rapid progress during recent years in the study of reading problems.

Illuminating facts concerning the rate of this development are presented in Table I. The entries show the number of studies, according to recent summaries (1 to 23 inclusive), that were published in England and America during each five-year interval since 1880. Only four of the studies listed were published prior to 1896. Between that date and 1910 interest in the study of reading problems increased materially. During the next five-year period, the number of investigations reported was greater than during the preceding thirty years. Since 1916 this country has witnessed an increase in the number of scientific studies of reading which is little less than phenomenal.

TABLE I
Number of Scientific Studies Relating to Reading Published in the United States and England since 1880

Five-Year Period	Number of Studies
1881-1885	1
1886-1890	1
1891-1895	2
1896-1900	10
1901-1905	6
1906-1910	14
1911-1915	49
1916-1920	151
1921-1925	274
1926-1930	490
1931-1935	534
1936-1939	419
Total	1951

Facts relating to the kinds of problems studied are even more significant than those relating to their number. More than half of the studies published prior to 1910 were laboratory studies relating to the psychology and physiology of reading. This is not surprising in view of the keen interest in such matters which prevailed in Europe during the latter half of the nineteenth century. Other problems that were studied related to children's interests in reading, vocabulary mastery, rhythm in oral reading, and the historical development of school readers. Two notable results of the studies prior to 1910 form the basis of present-day reforms in teaching reading; namely, the clear-cut distinction between oral reading and silent reading and the recognition of individual differences in reading habits and needs.

The period from 1911 to 1920 may be characterized as one of transition. It marks the beginning of broader interest in the scientific study of reading and clearer recognition of the need of applying objective methods to classroom problems. An examination of the studies made between 1911 and 1913, inclusive, shows, for example, that they related to such issues as methods of learning to read, the relative merits of different methods of beginning reading, the value of phonics, the content of courses of study in reading, and the amount and quality of reading material in various schools and grades. The explanation of this trend in interest is found in the fact that the results of the studies made in the early period challenged the validity of prevailing methods of teaching and suggested numerous practical problems for investigation.

A second significant fact concerning the transitional period is the introduction of new instruments of investigation. During 1914 and 1915 two thirds of the studies reported related to the organization, standardization, and application of reading tests. Through their use it became possible to study under classroom conditions, the reading habits, achievements, and difficulties of large groups of children. By the beginning of 1916 scientists, school surveyors, administrators, and teachers in various parts of the country were actively engaged in measuring the results of instruction in reading, in comparing achievement in oral and silent reading, in determining the effect on progress in reading of different conditions and teaching procedures, and in studying the errors and difficulties of individual children. These examples suggest merely the general character of the problems which began to command attention as early as 1920.

The current period of unprecedented interest in reading problems has at least three significant characteristics. The first is the tremendous increase in the number of studies reported. The second is the rapid increase in the range of problems studied. Throughout the last two decades the field of investigation has broadened steadily until it now includes problems that arise before children enter school, that command attention at various levels of general education, and that merit attention at the college and university levels. Equally significant is the fact that scientific methods are being used widely to study reading problems that have their origin in the home, in the library, and in adult life in general, as well as in the school. Indeed, it may be said that basic questions have arisen during recent years concerning practically all the major aspects of reading of which we are aware today, and vigorous effort has been made to secure a clear understanding of them through the use of objective methods.

The fact that many types of specialists have contributed generously of their time and energy to the study of reading problems has resulted in the accumulation of an extensive and varied literature. The findings of each study reported has raised more new problems than it has solved. As a result, we are far more conscious today than formerly of the complexity of the reading problems which we face and are far less certain of the answers to many of them. The fact is now widely recognized that scientific studies in this field must continue on a broad scale if reading is to serve ultimately its broadest function as a means of personal development, scholastic success, and social betterment.

But the progress achieved thus far is not without serious limitations. Unfortunately much of the scientific work relating to reading has been fragmentary in character. As pointed out by Brownell (10: No. 10),[1] the investigator frequently attacks an isolated problem, completes his study of it, and suggests that he will continue his research at some later time but often fails to do so. In the second place, there is little or no coordination of effort among research workers in the field of reading. In the third place, many of the studies reported have been conducted without adequate controls. Furthermore, interpretations are often based on traditional concepts of learning and as a result are not widely applicable today. Nevertheless, much of the evidence available is so significant that it serves as a valuable guide in reorganizing and improving instruction in reading at all levels and in defining with greater clarity the function of reading in contemporary life.

Organization of Article

The material in this article has been organized under the following heads:

  I. Sociology of Reading
 II. Nature of Reading and Basic Processes Involved
III. Factors Related to Growth in Reading
 IV. Interest in Reading

[1]In this documentation "No. 10" designates the tenth reference in item 10 in the bibliography at the end of this article.

V. Reading Readiness
VI. Aims, Organization, and Time Allotment of Reading in the Grades
VII. Nature, Content, and Grade Placement of Reading Materials
VIII. Methods of Teaching
IX. Reading in the Content Fields
X. Diagnosis and Remedial Teaching
XI. Hygiene of Reading

I. Sociology of Reading

Because reading is in final analysis an instrument of social progress, it will be appropriate to consider first some of its social relationships and implications. Accordingly, the discussion that follows is concerned with a group of problems relating to the sociology of reading.

Motives for Reading at Different Periods in History

The fact that the motives for reading in society at large have differed notably at various periods in history has been emphasized by Lamport (31). As a result of extended studies of traditional purposes for reading, he found that "training for citizenship—for the contemplation of philosophy or the practice of oratory—dominated Greek and Roman reading." Obviously cultural and utilitarian motives developed side by side. The religious motive for reading attained great prominence in the Middle Ages as children and adults were prepared for service in the church, and after the Reformation as a means of enabling laymen to understand the Scriptures. During the sixteenth and seventeenth centuries reading was used widely as a means of acquiring useful information. Only rarely before the nineteenth century did writers abroad emphasize the pleasure which the reader might derive from books.

Significant changes in motives for reading in this country have been identified and described by Smith (36). During the early colonial days, for example, reading activities were dictated largely by religious motives. This was particularly true in Massachusetts where practically all the materials read had religious or moral implications. The birth of the nation in 1776 gave rise to new motives for reading. Whereas the Church had earlier been chiefly concerned in inculcating religious motives, the major aims of the State now were to promote solidarity and national unity. The development of this new interest created strong and impelling motives for reading both in and out of school.

By 1825 national leaders as well as educators began to emphasize the need for preparing the great mass of our citizens to discharge their civic duties intelligently. As Smith rightly points out, the speeches and writings of that time were "saturated" with this underlying social motive. It is not surprising, therefore, to find that the chief motives for reading during the middle half of the nineteenth century were to secure (a) broad knowledge of the world and (b) understanding essential to good citizenship. About 1885 a new movement began to express itself. Its chief aim was to broaden the cultural life of the nation and to promote interest in the better types of literature. It found expression in society at large in the development of libraries and in the increase in the number of magazines published. In harmony with this trend the literary ideal dominated the teaching of reading between 1895 and 1910.

Since 1920 important economic and social developments have increased notably the need for broad understanding and discriminating insight concerning both personal and social problems. As a result young people and adults have made increasingly wide use of various sources of information—the press, the radio, the motion pictures, and the public forum—in attempting to understand and adjust themselves to new conditions. Furthermore, pressure groups and other agencies have been very active in developing attitudes and in promoting action that seriously threaten our democratic form of society. "As a result, the social significance of reading, as well as that of other means of informing or influencing the public has been greatly increased during recent years" (34: 10). It is reasonable to conclude, therefore, that from early times to the present reading has not only been a vital force in social life but has also reflected the changing needs, aspirations, and ideals of the social groups served.

Varied Purposes for Reading In Contemporary Life

Although the need for social enlightenment and broad understanding is a dominant characteristic of contemporary life, studies made since 1920 (1: 9) reveal a wide variety of purposes for reading among adults. The following list is typical but by no means exhaustive: "to keep informed concerning current events; to secure specific information of value in making plans; to learn more about events or problems of special interest; to secure the opinions of others concerning civic, social, or industrial problems; to keep in touch with business or professional developments; to secure suggestions concerning efficient methods of doing work; to determine important items in correspondence, messages, and instructions; to follow directions; to advance in one's field of work; to broaden one's range of information; to keep the mind stimulated with important things to think about; to develop a broad outlook on life; to secure pleasure during leisure hours; to satisfy curiosity."

The foregoing list should be supplemented by the findings of Waples (15: No. 89) who studied the social uses of print during the depression. The major purposes identified were: "to follow the news," "to find evidence," "to experience thrills," "to improve vocational competence," and "to defend class interests." The modes of reading adopted were characterized as "uncritical," "partisan," and "highly critical." In commenting on these different modes of reading, Waples pointed out the fact that different groups of readers passed from one to another of them "at different times and in a different sequence." Because of the broad social implications of these facts schools face a major responsibility today in establishing appropriate reading attitudes and habits.

Increase in the Amount of Reading

Facts concerning the amount of reading material published and read in this country during recent years are as significant as those relating to motives for reading. Data assembled by Judd (1: 10) showed that from 1850 to 1880 the per cent of increase in the number of issues of newspapers and periodicals published parallel closely the percentage of increase in the population. From 1880 to 1910, however, the number of issues of newspapers and periodicals increased more than 500 per cent. During the same period the increase in population was less than 100 per cent. In respect to the amount of library reading Parsons (1: 10) reported facts for Chicago which showed that in 1880 the population was 503,298 and the public library circulation 306,751. In 1920 the population was 2,701,705 and the library circulation was 7, 651,928. As compared with 1880, the population had increased at least 5 times and the library circulation more than 25 times.

More recent studies showed that the amount of reading material published continued to increase rapidly until 1930. During the next five years the number of copies of books, pamphlets, magazines, and daily and Sunday newspapers, as shown by Waples (15: No. 89) decreased appreciably as a result of the depression. During the same period, however, the amount of library reading increased rapidly, "because enforced leisure, prolonged idleness, and participation in educational activities all serve as an impetus for immediate reading and study" (12: No. 44, p. 3-4). When all the data available are considered, the fact is clear that America is rapidly becoming a nation of readers and that the responsibility of the schools to teach pupils to read intelligently becomes greater each year.

Wide Variations in Amount of Reading among States

Unfortunately the reading proclivities described above do not exist to the same degree in the various states and sections of the country. For example, data compiled by Stone (6: No. 47) showed that the number of inhabitants per daily paper varied in 1925 from 1.4 in the District of Columbia to 18.1 in Mississippi; that the inhabitants per magazine in the case of 47 leading magazines varied from 1.8 for California to 12.5 for Mississippi; and that the library circulation of books per capita varied from 4.8 in Massachusetts to .18 in Arkansas. These variations are typical of those found at both earlier and later dates. They assume large significance in view of the findings of Reeder (1: 11) to the effect that a high correlation exists between the rank of states in amount of reading and their rank on such bases as intelligence, the efficiency of their school systems, their productivity "as determined by agricultural and manufactured goods produced," and the extent to which they furnish national leaders, as shown by the names recorded in "Who's Who in America."

Studies of the causal factors involved show that the amount of reading done varies with such items as the history and wealth of a community or region, the character of its people, their attitudes, beliefs, and ideals, the accessibility of libraries and books, the extent of literacy, and the nature of the major activities in which people engage. Before any region or state can define clearly and accurately the nature of its reading and adult education problems, intensive studies should be made of the various factors that influence adult reading habits.

Reading Proclivities among Individuals

Of large social significance is the fact that the reading proclivities of individuals within communities vary to a surprising extent. At one extreme are those who read widely along many lines; at the other extreme are those who read little or not at all. Such differences suggest wide variations among the people of a community in their familiarity with current events, local, state, and national issues, and the cultural heritage of the race and in their insight and understanding of the personal and vocational problems which they face.

The results of community surveys (6: No. 47, p. 262) show clearly that the amounts read by individuals vary with conditions. For example, "adults who have had wide educational advantages read far more, as a rule, than those of more limited training. This is to be expected since educated people have broader interests which can be satisfied through reading. They are also thrown daily in contact with people who are well read, and they consequently find it necessary to read extensively themselves in order to be equally well informed" (6: No. 47, p. 262).

The amount read differs widely also with occupational groups. Those who belong to professional groups, for example, read as a rule about twice as much daily as those belonging to clerical groups and almost three times as much as those belonging to trade and labor groups. Other factors, such as previous educational advantages and present social contacts, complicate apparent relationships between occupation and amount of reading. Furthermore, "married people devote a larger amount of time to reading than unmarried; older people devote somewhat more time to reading than younger people, although the difference is not pronounced; men read more than women, particularly among the married groups" (6: No. 47, p. 263). Because of the complexity of the problem, it is impossible to draw conclusions concerning the relative importance of the various factors that now influence the reading habits of individuals. Additional studies are needed of the factors and conditions within the individual, in his home, and in his broader environment that influence reading habits, and to determine their relative significance for different types of individuals.

Character of the Material Read

In final analysis the kind and quality of the material read is of far greater importance than the amount of reading that is done. For purposes of clarity the discussion that follows will consider separately facts relating to newspaper, magazine, and book reading. Various studies provide evidence that newspapers are read almost universally. It would be valid to assume, therefore, that they might be one of the most powerful agents of modern society for promoting individual development and social progress. Unfortunately, however, the reading of newspapers fails in many respects to achieve these ends as fully as might be expected. This is due to the large percentage of space devoted to crime and strictly sensational news.

As compared with the last quarter of the nineteenth century, there has been during recent years a marked "decrease in news, both political and social, and in the amount of space given to editorials, letters, and opinions. This decrease in editorials and opinion has been attributed by some to 'the tendency toward standardization of thought' and to the 'contempt' on the part of owners of the press 'for the views of readers' and an 'unwillingness to give dissenting opinion a chance to express itself' " (6: No.

47, p. 265). Evidence of the preference of many newspaper readers for trite and sensational news is found in the large circulation of tabloids and in the pronounced tendency on the part of readers to direct their attention to cartoons, the sport section, and items relating to personal violence and disaster. Such facts lend support to the conclusion that much of the newspaper reading in contemporary life is based on brief unrelated accounts concerning items of minor importance. In fact, one of the major educational problems which the nation faces today relates to the need for greater interest in types of reading of large personal and social significance.

Analyses of the contents of magazines show that they include materials varying all the way from modern classics to the cheapest type of sensational materials. Studies of the circulation of magazines show that the eight or ten which are usually recognized as superior in character have relatively small circulations and that the so-called popular middle-grade magazines are published in greatest numbers. There is general agreement among investigators that the current-events type of magazine contains material that is more cosmopolitan and valuable than is true of the typical newspaper. Inquiries made among children and parents reveal the fact that a surprisingly large number of magazines of the cheap sensational type "are subscribed for regularly or purchased at the newsstand. The prominence of these magazines on the home library table suggests the urgent need of campaigns among adults to elevate their tastes and to stimulate interest in magazines of a better class" (6: No. 47, p. 266).

With respect to books fiction is without doubt the most popular although biography and travel are read widely. Of large significance is the fact that the specific type of books preferred varies from year to year. Furthermore, popular interest is influenced by a wide range of factors. For example, "sales increase notably if reference is made to a book in a news column, if a public speaker makes a favorable comment concerning a book, or if an editorial appears in which a book is referred to favorably....Furthermore, such events as a great criminal trial will create increased demand for books on psychology, psychoanalysis and medicine, or a hunting trip by a prominent man will stimulate interest in books relating to hunting, travel, and foreign countries" (6: No. 47, p. 266). Additional evidence that the selection of books may be easily influenced is found in the large increase in the number of books read following a "book fair" or a drive for better books. The need is urgent for additional studies to determine methods and agencies through which increased interest in good books can be stimulated among various elements in our population. The fact that more books are not read is due to lack of interest in reading, to failure to locate simple books relating to themes in which adults are interested, and to the lack of books in many communities.

Efforts to Classify Reading Materials in Qualitative Terms

Since the kinds of materials read by different elements in our population differ widely, students of reading and of sociology have become increasingly interested of late in techniques of evaluating reading materials. Wert (14: No. 88), for example, attempted to develop a technique for determining levels of group reading. He assumed, first, that "the quality of all reading done by a group can be noted by the quality of the magazines read by that group" and second, that "the quality of one magazine is higher than another if the average reader" of the former "is higher in scholastic aptitude,... ranks higher in English proficiency,... shows a greater knowledge of contemporary affairs." By giving a battery of tests covering these items and by securing information concerning magazines read regularly and occasionally, he classified magazines into different levels of quality. Using the *Saturday Evening Post* as a "base quality," he developed an index number for each of 39 magazines. These ratings were then applied to different groups with such results as the following: "entering freshmen present an average reading level coincident with the *Saturday Evening Post,* the quality increasing throughout the college period" and then decreasing somewhat for adults in the community. Although some of the basic assumptions underlying Wert's procedures have not been validated, his study in general is very interesting and suggestive. It indicates the possiblity of developing techniques which may be of great assistance in evaluating what is read by different individuals and groups.

Relation of Available Materials to What Readers Want to Read About

In many of the recent studies of reading the fact has been pointed out that adults often do not read because materials are not available relating to the topics in which they are most interested. Striking evidence in support of this view was secured by Waples and Tyler (8: No. 111, p. 63) who found that "the books said to circulate most widely contain only one fifth of the subjects of most interest to eight or more of sixteen typical groups. That is to say, the interest of the sixteen selected groups in the twenty-three widely circulating topics is relatively low. The implication of this fact is that publishers, booksellers, and librarians might all benefit by knowing what other topics than those treated in popular books particular groups of adults prefer to read about."

Readability of Adult Materials

One of the reasons why many adults read so little is that much of the available material is too difficult to read easily (12: No. 44). A majority of adults rank at about the seventh-grade level or below in reading ability, while more than half of the material relating to adult interests cannot be read with ease and understanding by those who rank as low as beginning seventh grade in reading ability. Obviously these facts have wide social and educational implications. If reading is to serve its largest function in promoting individual development and social progress, either the reading ability of adults must be greatly increased in the future or far more material relating to adult interests must be prepared which can be read easily by those of limited reading ability.

In recognition of the foregoing facts various investigators (14: No. 39), including Dale and Tyler, Ojemann, McClusky, Vogel and Washburne, Gray and Leary, and Bryson, have carried on informal and controlled experimentation to determine the factors which influence readability. Of the structural elements studied by Gray and Leary, the following ranked high for all readers: average sentence length; percentage of easy words; number of words not known to 90 per cent of sixth-grade pupils; number of easy words; number of different hard words; minimum syllabic sentence length; number of explicit sentences; and number of first-, second-, and third-person pronouns. Without doubt the most challenging problems which investigators face in the further study of readability relate to the nature of the concepts included and the form of their presentation. Through the cooperation of all individuals and agencies concerned with the readability of printed materials, notable progress should be made in the near future both in preparing readable material for different types of readers and in identifying desirable books for specific readers.

Steps in Further Developing a Sociology of Reading

In concluding the report of a study of the effect of the depression on reading Waples suggested that "a sociology of reading will develop in so far as we learn *who reads what and why over consecutive periods of time*" (15: No. 89, p. 200). This proposal is based on two assumptions: "that what people read can be used to describe their attitudes and that the people whose attitudes are of most interest to sociology in the study of public opinion actually read enough to reveal their attitudes." If these assumptions are accepted, the further development of a sociology of reading involves three major tasks: "*a*) to determine the most significant facts concerning the reading of any population group, *i.e.* facts that best describe their total reading behavior and which also bear most directly upon important hypotheses of social science; *b*) to devise valid indexes of the facts that reflect central tendencies, indexes which will enable social scientists to apply reading data to their own problems; *c*) to arrange for the continuous recording of such facts for adequate samples of the reading population in relation to social changes in the population at large" (15: No. 89, p. 201).

II. Nature of Reading and Basic Processes Involved

The fact was emphasized repeatedly in the preceding section that schools face major responsibilities if reading is to serve its broadest function as a means of personal development and social progress. This in turn requires a clear understanding of the nature of reading and of the basic processes involved. Accordingly this section will review briefly three concepts of reading that differ radically in character and will summarize at some length the results of studies relating to the motor and mental processes involved in reading.

1. Three Concepts of Reading

The nature of the reading act has been variously described by different writers and investigators (34). According to one view reading is primarily a process of perceiving or recognizing written or printed symbols. Such a conception gives large emphasis to accuracy in recognizing words, to the amount recognized at each fixation of the eyes, to the rate at which words and phrases are recognized, to the rhythmical progress of perceptions along the lines, and to the return sweep of the eyes from the end of one line to the beginning of the next. Because of the relative ease with which these phases of reading can be measured numerous objective studies of them have been made during recent years.

A much broader concept of reading assumes that it involves not only the fluent, accurate recognition of words but also the fusion of the specific meanings represented into a chain of related ideas. Early studies in this field directed attention to two important aspects of reading; namely, rate and comprehension. During the last three decades investigators have studied widely the achievement of pupils in these respects, the factors that influence rate and comprehension, and the methods of increasing efficiency in them.

A third concept of reading assumes that the reader not only apprehends the author's meaning but also reflects on the significance of the ideas presented, evalutes them critically, and makes application of them in the solution of problems. This concept of reading is often criticized on the ground that it includes much that psychologists and educators have commonly called *thinking*. It is defended by many who maintain that reading is not a psychologically unique process, but rather "a complex of mental activities having much in common with other complex operations and also some elements that are unique" (34: 28). Since many of the purposes that take the reader to the printed page require critical evaluation or the application of the ideas apprehended, or both, it seems reasonable to include them in any broad concept of reading that may be adopted.

The fact that reading has been conceived narrowly by some investigators and broadly by others suggests that great care must be observed in comparing the results of different studies. Furthermore, it is necessary to have clearly in mind an investigator's concept of reading before reacting critically to his recommendations. Obviously reading is a very complex art; furthermore, the need is urgent for a clear understanding of all that is involved in efficient reading. In summarizing pertinent studies in the sections that follow, reference will be made first to those which relate to the motor processes in reading and second to those which relate to the mental processes involved.

2. Motor Processes in Reading

The chief motor processes in reading may be classified under three headings; namely, visual, vocal, and extraneous.

Visual

The oculomotor processes are associated directly with the movements of the eyes. Whereas it was formerly believed that the eyes moved in a continuous sweep from left to right across the page, early investigations (30) showed that they proceed from left to right in a series of quick, short movements and fixation pauses and then return to the left in one quick, usually unbroken movement, with fixation near the beginning of the next line. The experiments of Erdmann, Dodge, and others led to the conclusion that clear vision does not occur during interfixation movements and as a result perception in reading takes place only during the pauses. The validity of these conclusions has been challenged of late, but no conclusive evidence to the contrary has as yet been presented.

The grosser movements of the eyes referred to above have been analyzed in greater detail by Schmidt (1: No. 329, p. 114) who identified several types of movements in both the horizontal and the vertical planes. Of major importance in the horizontal plane are the interfixation movements, including refixations either to the left or the right, and the return sweep from the end of one line to the beginning of the next. "The most striking characteristic of these movements appears in the fact that the two eyes do not cover equal distances in executing them, the leading eye (in space) passing invariably over a greater extent than the eye which follows. Such movement implies divergent adjustment."

In connection with the fixation pauses, three distinct types of eye movements in the horizontal plane have been identified. "The first involves a gradual convergent movement of the eyes, this being most strongly in evidence in the case of the initial fixation pause of each line; the second type represents a rapid movement of both eyes at the beginning of certain fixation pauses in a direction opposite to that of the preceding connective movement; the third type involves isolated irregular excursions of the eyes in either direction, rarely more than one occurring in connection with any one fixation, such movement being due in all probability to lack of muscular balance" (1: No. 329, p. 114-15).

As indicated by the foregoing statements, a line of print is read during several fixations of the eye from left to right. In addition, there is a greater or smaller number of regressive or backward movements to refixate on a word or phrase. As a result of a critical review of the literature relating to such movements, Tinker (14: No. 82, p. 8) concluded that "one type of regression is to correct inaccuracies in the location of the first fixation at the left end of a line after the backsweep from the end of preceding line." Other regressions within the line are "to achieve more adequate perception and apprehension. According to Dearborn, ... the better readers soon tend to form 'shortlived motor habits' in which about the same number of pauses are made per line for that particular material. Generally the first pause in the line is longest, the last somewhat shorter, and those between still shorter."

The first and last fixations in a line are usually indented more or less from the ends of the line. Quoting again from Tinker (14: No. 82, p. 9) "Huey discovered that 78 to 82 per cent of the printed line was covered by the fixations. The findings of Dearborn are similar. Tinker found that this varied with the type of reading: 84 per cent of the line was transversed by the eye in reading prose, 89 per cent in algebra, and 99 per cent in lines of formulas. As reading and study become more analytical, therefore, more of the line is covered by the fixations." Tinker also reviewed the results of previous studies and contributed new data concerning the relative amount of time devoted to fixation movements and pauses. His summary indicated that approximately 94 per cent of the reading time is devoted to pauses and 6 per cent to fixation movements. As the reading becomes more analytical an increasingly small proportion of the time is devoted to movements.

The eye movements in the vertical plane are similar in certain respects to those in the horizontal plane. According to Schmidt (1: No. 329, p. 115), there is first "a gradual upward movement of the eyes in connection with the interfixation movements and the return sweep, this being indicative of divergent adjustment." In connection with the fixation pauses there are two types of movements. "The first represents a downward movement of the eyes during fixation, this being indicative of convergent adjustment." The second type includes "isolated irregular excursions of the eyes" due largely to lack of muscular balance. In addition, slight "compensatory eye-movements" were identified in both planes but were not definitely characterized. As indicated by the foregoing comments many of the smaller movements of the eyes are closely related "to divergent and convergent binocular adjustment." Obviously the inadequacies inherent in the more elementary or grosser forms of ocular behavior "are overcome by the higher forms of binocular adjustment" (1: No. 329, p. 117). As will be indicated in a later section, inability to make the necessary ocular adjustments may be a cause of reading difficulty.

Vocal

By virtue of its very nature, oral reading involves very definite vocal reactions. Even in silent reading, vocalization is more or less pronounced in the case of many individuals.

The rate at which the various adjustments involved in vocalization are acquired has important implications in respect to both oral and silent reading. Fluent oral reading is possible, for example, when meanings are apprehended quickly and when the muscles that control the organs of speech respond quickly and effectively to stimuli from printed symbols. In order to determine the rate at which ability to articulate matures, Gray (1: No. 125) and Judd (1: No. 204) asked pupils at different grade levels to repeat digits as rapidly as they could for a period of time, such as 30 seconds. The results indicated that increase in vocal facility is very rapid in the lower grades, much slower in the middle grades, and insignificant in the upper grades. Wide variations in the rate of articulation at each grade level were noted. When the rate of articulation and the rate of recognition in reading were compared it was found that the latter surpassed the former at about the fourth-grade level. Judd concluded that when pupils reach this stage of development increased emphasis should be given to silent reading. As methods of teaching improve, an increasing percentage of children learn somewhat earlier in the grades to recognize words more rapidly than they can pronounce them.

The extent to which the organs of speech are involved in silent reading has challenged keen interest among investigators for decades. Observations reveal the fact that most pupils who are learning to read move their lips to a greater or less extent when reading silently. As they become more proficient in reading, these movements are very much abbreviated and in time disappear altogether among good readers. In the case of less-fluent readers they often persist throughout life. Many of the vocal accompaniments of silent reading, however, cannot be observed directly. They take the form of minor or incipient movements in the larynx, in the tip or base of the tongue, in the palate, or in other parts of the vocal apparatus. These movements may occur for each word or, as Judd has pointed out, for a group of words representing an idea. Because of the nature of these movements it has been difficult to secure adequate records of them. Curtis, as quoted by Gray (1: No. 125, p. 157), "procured objective records of the movements of the larynx by placing a sensitive tambour over this organ." A record of the movements was made on a moving drum. He found that in 15 out of 20 cases movements were recorded. Failure to secure records in 5 cases was attributed to lack of refinement in the recording instrument. In commenting on these findings, Gray pointed out the fact that it was possible that movements occurred in other parts of the vocal apparatus.

Other experimenters using different methods have secured evidence of the presence of incipient movements of the vocal apparatus in silent reading. The data available do not prove conclusively that they occur among all readers or are essential. Final conclusions must await the development of more refined recording instruments. Those who favor the view that movements of the vocal apparatus are an invariable accompaniment of silent reading do so on the theory that meanings and language are so closely related in consciousness that the recognition of meaning in reading cannot occur without the reinstatement of the movements involved in vocalization. Others hold to the view that the presence of vocal movements in silent reading is a by-product of current methods of teaching pupils to read. The normal method of teaching reading introduced recently in the Chicago Public Schools is based on this assumption (14: No. 54). In the light of the evidence available, the burden of proof rests on those who maintain that movements of the vocal apparatus are not essential and reduce efficiency in silent reading.

Brief reference should be made next to the relation between breathing and oral reading. In this connection the length of the expiration period is very important. It is during this part of the breathing act that oral expression occurs. Experience shows that if the expirations are short, the reading is likely to be jerky; if they are prolonged, the reader is likely to give the impression of running down. According to C.T. Gray (1: No. 125, p. 171) the length of the expiration period should "vary with the material read, the inflection, force, and other factors which influence the reading." His studies show clearly the respiration "may proceed in a way to be of direct assistance in expression or it may go on in a way which gives every evidence that control and adjustment are lacking." One of the functions of a good teacher is to help pupils learn to control respiration while reading so that it aids rather than interferes with oral interpretation.

Extraneous
Associated with reading are a number of extraneous movements, such as changes in facial expression, movements of the head forward or backward or from side to side, lowering or raising of one or both shoulders, or other bodily attitudes. C.T. Gray (1: No. 125) associates such movements largely with poor readers and claims that they may represent a lack of proper adjustment to the reading situation. Huey (30: 167), on the other hand, takes the position that some of these movements furnish "the very body of much that we call meaning." Undoubtedly both explanations are applicable. Experience teaches that poor readers do engage in many extraneous movements as they encounter difficulty in reading; we know also that many very good readers give evidence of distinct head and facial movements while reading. As pointed out by Judd (1: No. 204), meanings arise out of reactions and are often closely associated with bodily attitudes and movements.

3. Mental Processes in Reading

Studies in the psychology of reading show that various mental, as well as motor, processes are involved. Because of their very nature they are much more difficult to identify and describe than are the motor processes. In the paragraphs that follow significant facts concerning the perception or recognition of words, the apprehension of the meaning of what is read, and the reader's reaction to or use of the ideas apprehended will be summarized briefly.

Perception or Recognition of Words

Essential aspects of word perception include the presence of written or printed symbols, attentive adjustment of the reader to these symbols, and the arousal of associations that result in the recognition of their identity, including their pronunciations or meanings or both. We are concerned for the moment with only the third of these aspects of word perception.

Practically all psychologists agree that when stimuli from printed words reach the visual centers of the brain associations are aroused which result in the recognition of pronunciations or meanings or both. A review of the literature relating to word perception reveals three distinct points of view concerning the source of these stimuli. One group of writers particularly those who favor an organismic concept of psychology, maintain and present evidence supporting the view that the context of the sentence, or large unit, provides the mental set and arouses the associations essential in the recognition of words. A second group maintains that the word is the unit of recognition in reading and that its total form is the distinguishing characteristic by which it is recognized. A third group attaches primary importance to letters or groups of letters variously known as "determiners"—"dominant" or "significant" letters or letter combinations. The fact should be noted, however, that the early group of investigators who favored this view considered the identification of letters merely as an aid in the perception of words and the recognition of meaning. Word recognition is attained in their judgment by combining the associations aroused with individual letters or groups of letters.

Analyses of the procedures adopted by mature readers indicate that the general context, the total form of the word, and detailed parts of words all function in word recognition. More than three decades ago Huey (30: 102-16) emphasized the fact that in the case of fluent reading the general form or outline of the word is a sufficient visual cue to its recognition. The aid supplied by the context "tips the balance in favor of the unitary recognition of the word.... With very familiar words, the letter recognitions are checked in their incipiency. With new words, the recognition of certain letters may quite complete itself before the whole word is known." It is evident, therefore, "that we read by phrases, words, or letters as we may serve our purpose best." Huey explained the fact, however, that there are very great individual differences, based, in part at least, "on the methods by which the reader has learned to read."

The foregoing discussion suggests questions concerning the extent to which perception is an analytic and a synthetic process. The function and place of analysis has been brought out clearly by Hamilton as a result of elaborate experimentation with children and adults. His findings indicate that in a majority of cases the general characteristics of a word are the clues by which it is recognized. "But when some unfavorable condition arises or when the words are strange or difficult, additional distinctions within the word are required, in which case the parts of the word must be brought more or less clearly to consciousness, according to the degree of complexity or unfamiliarity.... The form of procedure may therefore be described as predominantly synthetic-analytic, the amount of analysis tending in general to decrease with growth in ability and with increasing familarity with the material read" (1: No. 155, p. 52-53).

As a result of recent experimentation Vernon (39) has described even more fully the nature of the perceptual process. She maintains that both the total word form and the distinguishing characteristics of a word are important. They are the elements which differentiate one word from another. She also identified (38: 118-19) four steps or stages in the perception of words: a) a vaguely perceived form or contour, with b) certain dominating or specific parts, which c) stimulate auditory or kinesthetic imagery, and d) arouse meaning. These stages are assumed to be present in all normal reading situations. The fact should be pointed out that experiments with children indicate that in the process of learning to read they are more concerned with the dominating parts of words than are adults whose reading habits are mature. With increase in familiarity with words less and less conscious attention to their details is necessary.

The foregoing statements may be supplemented to advantage by more detailed facts concerning the perceptual process. According to Tinker (14: No. 82, p. 8-9) "the first pause seems to involve a general survey through the aid of peripheral vision of at least the first part of the line.... Extra foveal vision, especially to the right of the fixation, yields premonitions of coming words and phrase forms as well as stimulating meaning premonitions. Word forms, indistinctly seen in peripheral vision, begin the perceptual process much in advance of direct fixation." As a result, the number and duration of fixations are decreased and the rate of reading increased.

As indicated by the results of various experiments, the amount recognized at each fixation of the eyes differs with such factors as the type of material used—numbers, geometrical forms, nonsense syllables, meaningful groups of words—and the reader's familiarity with them. Furthermore, the average amount recognized at each fixation in reading is distinctly less, as a rule, than the average amount of the same type of material recognized at one fixation in a short-exposure apparatus. This is due largely to the fact that in the latter case the reader has time to recall and organize the various impressions received before attention is directed to a new unit. The fact that the span of recognition is not as large, on the average, as the perceptual span has stimulated both investigators and teachers to develop methods of increasing the span of recognition which in turn greatly improves the efficiency of the reader.

Inasmuch as most of the studies of perception in reading have dealt with only specific aspects of the total problem, one should accept cautiously the viewpoint of any single investigator concerning the nature of the perceptual process. Each of scores of studies in this field add something of importance to an understanding of the perception of words. The critical summaries by such writers as Huey (30), Vernon (38), and Tinker (14: No. 82) provide the best sources now available for a comprehensive picture of findings and needed research.

Apprehension of Meaning

Only a limited number of studies have related specifically to the mental processes involved in the apprehension of the meaning of what is read. All investigators agree that these processes are numerous and complex. The fact is also widely recognized that the two basic processes in comprehension are first the arousal of meaningful associations with words and groups of words as stimuli from the retina reach the visual centers of the brain and, second, the fusion of these meanings into a chain of related ideas. In the first of these steps the chief resource of the reader is his background of related experience. Only in so far as the reader's experiences relate in some form or other to the concepts or situations to which the author refers can the reader comprehend what is read. It follows that a reader's meaning vocabulary in terms of extent and richness is of large importance. In fact, it correlates more highly with comprehension than any other factor studied thus far except intelligence (1: No. 179).

In the act of reading, however, one cannot always rely on the meanings which he has previously attached to specific words. This is due to the fact that they are often used by the writer in a new or different sense. As a result the reader must search, sometimes quite vigorously, for the specific meanings implied by the words read. The essence of this phase of the reading act, according to Richards (35), is to select and combine relevant items of experience that are implied by the immediate context, by the author's mood, tone, or intention, and by everything the reader knows that makes clear the meaning of a passage. Not infrequently, however, these sources of information are inadequate and the reader must make use of glossaries, dictionaries, encyclopedias, textbooks, and even periodicals, movies, radio broadcasts, pictures, or direct contact with reality in an effort to discover appropriate meanings.

As meanings are aroused or discovered, they are so fused or related in the mind of the reader that the general meaning of the passage read is understood. According to Huey (30), James, and others the various elements of meaning are held before consciousness until the total meaning of the passage is understood. As a result it is possible for the reader to accept or modify the meanings which he first attached to particular words before using them in deriving the total meaning of a sentence or longer unit. The extent and variety of the mental activity involved in this aspect of reading has been described by Thorndike as a result of detailed studies of the processes involved in reading: "It consists in selecting the right elements of the situation and putting them together in the right relations, and also with the right amount of weight or influence or force for each. The mind is assailed as it were by every word in the paragraph. It must select, repress, soften, emphasize, correlate and organize, all under the influence of the right mental set or purpose or demand" (1: No. 377, p. 329).

The studies referred to above also led Thorndike to conclude that "reading an explanatory or argumentative paragraph in his (the pupil's) textbooks on geography or history or civics, and (though to a less degree) reading a narrative or description, involves the same sort of organization and analytic action of ideas as occur in thinking of supposedly higher sorts" (1: No. 377, p. 331).

One of the possible implications of the statement that meanings must be selected and organized in the light of the "right mental set or purpose or demand" is that the mental processes involved in reading vary with the purpose that takes the reader to the printed page. Evidence supporting this assumption was secured by Judd and Buswell who photographed the eye movements of 20 subjects. These subjects were asked to read a newspaper account a) rapidly merely to find out what it was about and b) carefully in order to answer questions about it. When the records were compared, it was found that in most cases careful reading was accompanied by a larger number of fixations, by longer duration of fixations, and by more regressive movements per line. These adjustments on the part of the reader indicated, according to the investigators, that the processes involved in reading vary with the purpose. They concluded, therefore, that a printed page turns out to be "a source of a mass of impressions which the active mind begins to organize and arrange with reference to some pattern which it is trained to work out. If the mind is fitting together the impressions so as to bring into high relief grammatical distinctions, the grouping of words and the distribution of emphasis will be according to one pattern. If the mind is intent on something wholly different from grammar, as, for example, the experiences which the author is trying to picture, the whole mental and physical attitude of the reader will be very different" (1: No. 203, p. 4).

The facts secured by Judd and Buswell also indicate that the processes involved in reading differ with the kind of material, for example, poetry and scientific exposition, and with its difficulty. Other experimenters have pointed out that familiarity with the material read modifies the processes involved in apprehending its meaning and the degree of concentration and effort required. The need is urgent for additional experiments which will identify more fully than has been done thus far the nature of the processes involved in securing a clear grasp of meaning and the extent and ways in which they are modified by the conditions under which one reads.

Reaction to the Use of the Ideas Apprehended

The discussion thus far has considered the processes involved in the recognition of words and the apprehension of meaning. As indicated earlier, the reader may engage also in a number of supplementary steps or processes of which the following are examples: drawing inferences, seeing implications, and judging the validity of the ideas presented; making judgments concerning the quality, effectiveness, or completeness of the author's presentations; comparing the views of different authors concerning the same issue; applying the ideas gained to new situations; using the information secured in the solution of personal and social problems; and integrating the ideas gained through reading with previous experience to acquire improved patterns of thinking and of action. Whether an individual compares the ideas read with previous experience, judges their validity, or applies them in the solution of a personal problem depends on his motives, purposes, attitudes, and interests at the time.

A comparison of what is involved in reading merely to discover an author's views and in reading to judge critically the views presented reveals a significant advantage of the latter aspect of reading. "In the former case a good reader makes use of every clue to meaning that he knows without letting any prejudice or bias of his own influence his decision.... As the views of the author are recognized, however, the reader evaluates them critically in the light of all that he knows, judges their validity or worth, and accepts or rejects them with discrimination.

Obviously in apprehending the meanings implied by the words used, the thinking of the reader is controlled by the author; in reacting critically to the ideas presented the reader controls his own thinking" (25: 27).

Unfortunately very little experimental evidence is available concerning the mental processes involved in the reader's reaction to or use of the ideas gained through reading. Obviously, they differ very little, if at all, from similar responses to what is seen or heard. In outlining procedures for the reader to adopt, specialists in reading have found it necessary to draw heavily on general psychological analyses and classroom observations of the steps desirable in achieving specific ends. The following description by Strang is illustrative of most of the information now available: "In reading to obtain proof on any point the student will first formulate the assumptions which are to be studied. Then he will select, as he reads, the ideas significantly related to the assumptions. He will search for evidence in support of or opposed to the assumptions and weigh each bit of evidence as he reads. If evidence accumulates against one of his original assumptions, he will change it. Finally, he will act upon the assumptions for which he has obtained proof. Judd has made a comprehensive analysis of the abilities required in scientific thinking which includes elements of observation, analysis, synthesis, selective recall, and imagination as well as ability to recognize the problem, judge the adequacy of data, discover essential relationships, and suspend judgment until enough reliable evidence is available on which to draw conclusions. Training in thinking is an essential part of a program for the improvement of reading on the higher levels of comprehension and application" (37: 47-48).

The foregoing statements make it clear that training pupils to react intelligently to and apply what is read is a very challenging responsibility. There is urgent need of carefully planned studies which aim to discover, first, the nature of the mental processes involved in reading for various purposes, second, the conditions which determine progress or growth on the part of the reader, and, third, the types of guidance which are most effective.

III. Factors Related to Growth in Reading

It is widely recognized that progress in acquiring efficient reading habits is influenced by various factors and conditions, such as the learner's stage of development, his interest in reading, and the amount of incentive and guidance afforded by his total environment. Interest in identifying such factors developed early in this century with the discovery of individual differences in achievement and rate of growth and has remained at a high level to the present time. In the paragraphs that follow an effort will be made to summarize the major findings of research concerning the factors associated with growth in different aspects of reading. Owing to the nature of the data reported in some of the investigations, it is often impossible to determine whether a given factor was merely associated with progress in reading or was causally related to it. Obviously more rigorous selection of data and further refinements in their statistical treatment are essential in future studies in this field.

Relation of Intelligence to General Progress in Reading

Because of its close relation to progress in every phase of reading, the mental capacity of the reader will be considered first. One of the early studies of the correlation between intelligence and silent reading achievement was reported by True (1: No. 386), who gave three intelligence tests and four silent reading tests to 218 pupils in grades 4 to 8 inclusive. The coefficients of correlation obtained varied from -.10 to +.87 with a mean of about +.50. The correlation was highest in the fourth grade, relatively high in the fifth and sixth grades, and somewhat lower in the seventh and eighth grades. The correlations were somewhat higher in the case of the group intelligence tests than in the case of the Stanford-Binet Intelligence Test. This was doubtless due to the fact that reading was involved to a greater or less extent in the group intelligence tests. Early studies at the college level also revealed relatively high correlations when group intelligence tests were involved (1: No. 407). The correlations differed widely, however, for different parts of the intelligence tests used, suggesting that certain mental functions may be far more influential in reading than others.

Recent studies have tended to be much more analytical and discriminating than earlier ones. For example, Leavell and Sterling (16: No. 70) found correlations between intelligence and such basic factors in reading as number of fixations, number of regresssions, duration of fixations, span of recognition, rate, and comprehension. The data secured showed "a fairly marked tendency" for the more intelligent children to do better in these various aspects of reading than the less intelligent. The size of the coefficients varied with the intelligence tests used. Furthermore, the differences between the superior and average intelligence groups were greater in more of the basic factors when the Kuhlman-Anderson Intelligence Test was used than when the Myers Mental Measure was used.

With very few exceptions all the studies which have been reported show a greater or less degree of positive correlation between general intelligence and reading achievement. The fact that reported correlations are generally not above .40 to .50 indicates that factors other than intelligence influence progress in reading. Variations in coefficients when different reading and intelligence tests were used are due to the fact that different aspects of reading and different combinations of mental functions were measured. The need is urgent for the development of more refined measures of intelligence and for a clearer definition of the mental functions involved. Equally important is the need for more discriminating measures of progress in different aspects of reading and of achievement in reading different types of material and in reading for different purposes.

Factors Related to Progress in Oral Reading

In a study involving 1050 primary grade pupils, Oglesby (1: No. 282) classified them into three groups on the basis of their intelligence scores. When oral reading tests were given it was found that the superior group usually, although not always, read the most rapidly, made the fewest errors, and attempted the hardest paragraphs. The fact that there was a large amount of overlapping indicated that factors other than intelligence influenced progress.

Studies made during the last twenty-five years have identified many other factors that influence progress in oral reading. Briefly stated, they are nationality, sex, economic conditions, methods of teaching, provision for individual differences, and the amount read. For example, girls on the average make more rapid progress in learning to read aloud than do boys; children coming from favorable economic conditions do better as a rule than less fortunate children; children who do much oral reading usually excel those who read little aloud; Jewish children who speak English make far more rapid progress as a rule than children of like attainments but belonging to other nationality groups. Additional factors and conditions which have frequently been associated with differences in progress but whose influence has not been so fully or objectively determined are school attendance, health, attitude of pupils toward reading, the ability of the teacher, the quality of the reading materials used, the amount of time devoted to reading, detailed techniques of teaching, the out-of-school experiences of pupils, and the amount and character of the kindergarten training received. Carefully planned studies are needed to determine the character of the influence exerted by these factors. Furthermore, studies should be made of various combinations of factors and conditions to determine which are most favorable to rapid progress.

Factors Related to Growth in Comprehension

Because of the large importance of comprehension in most reading activities, the factors which influence its development merit careful consideration. A survey of the literature relating to such factors reveals two types of studies. The first and most frequent type was so organized that little more was achieved than to identify factors that were associated with differences in comprehension. Suggestive as such studies are they do not show whether given factors actually promote or retard growth in comprehension. Many of the studies made in connection with public-school surveys are of this general character. The second and most valuable type aimed to determine the relation of specific factors to progress in comprehension. Some of these studies were carefully organized; others failed to control or hold constant some of the variables. In such cases it was not always clear that a causal relationship actually existed. Nevertheless, the evidence now available concerning certain factors is sufficiently dependable to justify tentative conclusions.

One of the most illuminating studies in this field was made by Hilliard (1: No. 170) who first identified through a survey of the literature of silent reading twelve factors that might influence comprehension. Six of them were eliminated from further study because satisfactory methods of isolating them could not be devised. An effort was then made to determine the relation to comprehension of the remaining six; namely, general intelligence, meaning vocabulary, rate of reading, ability to reproduce material read, lip movement and articulation, and ability to organize. Several tests of each of these factors were given. The results attained through the method of partial correlation showed that there was positive correlation between comprehension and each of five of them. The zero order of correlations reaffirmed this relationship and showed the following order of importance among them: "intelligence, vocabulary, organization, rate, reproduction." Later studies have verified repeatedly the existence of a positive relationship in the case of intelligence and vocabulary. Questions arise concerning the nature of the relationship in the case of ability to organize and to reproduce and in the case of rate of reading.

A review of all evidence available shows that some of the factors which influence comprehension are inherent in the reader, such as general intelligence, meaning vocabulary, background of related experience, interest in reading, and to a limited extent, race, nationality, and sex. Other factors are pedagogical in nature, such as the training and experience of the teacher, a clear definition of objectives in teaching comprehension, a vigorous program of instruction and pupil guidance, and the amount of reading required. Still other factors are inherent in the material read, such as its readability and the skillful use of pictures in the text (13: No. 40). Wise utilization of these findings may materially affect practice in the future in organizing instruction and in providing guidance that aims to improve comprehension.

Factors Related to Improvement in Meaning Vocabulary

Because of the large importance of meaning vocabulary in reading, Gray and Holmes (15: No. 35) made an extended study of the literature on reading to identify factors that are related to its development. The evidence secured indicated that growth in meaning vocabulary is correlated more or less closely with intelligence, the nature of the instruction given, the experience and cultural influences of the pupils, and interest in the meanings of words. Other factors considered but which proved to have little or no correlation with growth in meaning vocabulary, or concerning which the evidence was not conclusive, were sex, the study of Latin, and amount of reading. One of the most encouraging facts revealed was the large influence exerted by the kind of instruction given.

Bonser, Burch, and Turner (1: No. 36), for example, compared the meaning vocabularies of pupils in two schools which differed widely in respect to the economic and social status of the families represented. The test scores showed clearly that the pupils of one school ranked significantly higher in meaning vocabularies than the pupils of the other although the former group was distinctly inferior in social and economic status and in intelligence scores. An analysis of various factors that might have influenced vocabulary development led to the conclusion that the chief difference between the two groups lay in the kind of instruction provided. Some of the important characteristics of the curriculum of the school which ranked highest in meaning vocabulary were described as follows (1: No. 36, p. 716): *a*) "Its subject matter is intimately and vitally related to everyday life—the schoolwork gives meaning and understanding of the daily activities of which the child himself is a part"; *b*) "the pupil is made to experience in his own life as much as possible of the race experience that is of fundamental value"; *c*) "the general plan of work calls for initiative and constant participation on the part of pupils comparable to that called forth by play and home life"; *d*) "the problem method of teaching, necessitating organization and clear, purposive thinking on the part of both teacher and pupils"; *e*) "because the matter presented is vitally related to the life of the children their expression is spontaneous, free, and adequate." The detailed facts presented lend support to the conviction of the experimenters that superiority was due largely to "vitalized content, social motive, and humanized method."

From the results of the various studies reported thus far it is obvious that four factors determine to a large extent the growth of a child's meaning vocabulary; namely, his capacity to learn, the character of his environment, the nature and development of his interests, and the kind of instruction provided. Further experimentation is needed in each of these fields to indicate clearly the nature and extent of the influence exerted.

Factors Related to Growth in Speed of Silent Reading

The large importance that attaches to speed of reading has stimulated many investigators to review the literature and to organize experimental studies to identify factors that influence it. As early as 1897 Quantz (1: No. 308) made an extended study of the factors that contribute to rapid reading. In his report, he emphasized the following: good "visual perception, practice as determined by the amount of reading from childhood on, power of concentration, mental alertness estimated by rapidity of original composition, scholarly ability as decided by college records." Quantz included in his list only those factors which analysis and judgment led him to believe were causally related to speed of reading.

Almost a quarter of a century later O'Brien (1: No. 280, p. 37-77) made an elaborate summary of experimental literature relating to speed of reading and concluded that the following factors influence the speed at which one reads: "practice in rapid silent reading," amount of vocalization, "training in perception," the kind and difficulty of subject-matter, purpose of reading, "concentration of attention," "ability to grasp the meaning," and "reaction time." These findings support some of the earlier conclusions of Quantz, particularly with reference to the value of practice in rapid silent reading, power of concentration, and training in perception. The fact that speed of reading varies with ability to concentrate and to grasp meaning led Quantz, O'Brien, and many later investigations to conclude that speed of reading is determined largely by the rate at which the mind can assimilate ideas rather than by the rate at which visual impressions are received and transferred to the brain.

Early investigators, such as Reudiger and Dearborn, held to the view that rapid readers in one type of material were usually rapid readers in other types also. Later experimenters, while recognizing the general validity of this view, have pointed out numerous exceptions which they attribute primarily to differences in interest and familiarity. For example, Pressey and Pressey (1: No. 305) reached the following conclusion based on the results of tests including poetry, scientific material, and stories: "A good reader in one type of subject-matter may very likely be a poor reader with other material." Furthermore, Judd and Buswell (1: No. 203) found that different kinds of passages, such as fiction, geography, rhetoric, easy verse, and algebra induced contrasting attitudes and distinctly different rates of reading on the part of individuals. Other investigations support the view that familiarity with the content of what is read and the simplicity of a passage definitely influence speed of reading.

Among the factors mentioned by O'Brien that influence speed of reading was "reaction time." Traxler (11: No. 90) studied this relationship in the case of five high-school groups, using "speed of association of ideas" as a measure of reaction time. He found that while the relationship was not high, it "was positive and high enough to be significant." He concluded that "there is ground for thinking that slow association rate may be so closely related to the retarded reading rate of some slow readers that the teacher should not utilize the usual methods to get them to read more rapidly."

When all of the evidence available is reviewed, it seems obvious that the following factors rank high in influencing speed of reading: the purpose of reading; the reader's familiarity with the content or related concepts; the kind of material read and its difficulty; the amount of thought given to the content while reading; the amount of lip movement while reading; the extent of practice in silent reading; and ability to grasp meaning readily as measured in part by reaction time, or rate of association of ideas.

Relation between Speed and Comprehension in Silent Reading

Before concluding the discussion of factors that influence progress in reading, the interrelations of speed and comprehension in silent reading should be considered. This issue has been the subject of many heated controversies. A critical review of the experimental literature in 1925 (1: 124-31) led to the following conclusions: *a*) There is positive correlation between speed and comprehension when "children read carefully" and when adults "read at their normal rates or rapidly." In both cases the relationship is by no means invariable. *b*) "The degree of correlation varies for children among school systems, schools, grades, and classes," and for adults among the different groups tested. *c*) The correlation between speed and comprehension in the case of children varies with such factors as the "kind of difficulty of passages," "the purpose of reading," and the measure of comprehension used. Mature readers, on the average, seem to grasp more of the ideas of a passage at a single reading if they read slowly than if they read at their normal rates. On the other hand, if the number of ideas per unit of time is the measure such persons make higher scores when reading rapidly.

Studies made during the last decade have been extremely critical of the techniques used in earlier investigations. For example, in 1932 Tinker (10: No. 77) reviewed the results of previous studies and presented new evidence. His studies led to the conclusion that dissimilar materials used in various reading tests do not yield comparable scores, that the many reading skills are somewhat independent, and that "the only adequate method of discovering the true relation between speed and comprehension" is to measure them "on the same or strictly comparable material." Data obtained by Tinker in harmony with this principle revealed very high intercorrelations and led him to conclude that "there is a close relation between speed and comprehension." Additional studies concerning the degree of correlation when reading different types of material, when reading materials of different levels of difficulty, and when reading for different purposes would be very illuminating. Further research is needed also to determine the effect of different types of teaching upon the degree of correlation between speed and comprehension and the reasons why the findings vary widely among different schools and classes and at different grade levels.

The fact that significant positive correlations have been found between speed and comprehension does not justify the practice of urging pupils to read as rapidly as they can. On the contrary, experiments show that increasing the rate of reading will most likely result in a decrease in comprehension. The practical procedure justified by the evidence now available is that pupils should be urged to read only as rapidly as they can achieve well the purpose that takes them to the printed pages.

IV. Interest in Reading

Studies relating to reading interests have been reported for at least fifty years. One of the earliest studies published appeared anonymously in the May, 1889, issue of *Education* under the title "What Do Pupils Read?" During the nineties at least seven studies were made of the reading interest of elementary- and secondary-school pupils and of adults. They were concerned largely with library withdrawals, favorite books of boys and girls, literature and characters that appealed most strongly, and changes in reading interests from childhood to adulthood.

During the period from 1900 to 1920 a relatively small number of studies of reading interests were published. The average was less than one a year. Jordan's comprehensive report (1: No. 198) in 1921 included a summary of twenty previous studies and two original experiments. From 1920 to 1929 interest in this field increased very rapidly. By 1929 Gray and Munroe (6: No. 47) reported almost a hundred studies of the reading interests of elementary and secondary pupils. During the following decade interest in this field continued to increase steadily and at present (1940) approximately two hundred published studies are available.

Many of the early investigators employed a questionnaire as the means of obtaining data relative to reading interests. Other methods include analysis of book withdrawals in libraries; observation of children in classrooms, in libraries, and at home; and conferences with readers. In a few cases the investigator has sought to determine under controlled conditions the preferences of pupils, or the effect of a selected procedure on growth in interest and in the expressed preferences of pupils. When properly organized, the experimental procedure is valid and highly productive, but it is exceedingly expensive of time and energy.

The data available in respect to most issues concerning reading interests have usually been secured in various ways and often without adequate controls; hence great care must be observed in drawing conclusions from them. The need is great for an extension and refinement of the techniques of investigation in this field and for the study of more problems under comparable conditions and through the use of corresponding techniques. Of even greater importance is the need for studies which can identify latent as well as developed interests and discriminate between basic interests and those which are the product of mere circumstance, such as the availability of books of particular types.

Some of the major findings and conclusions are presented under two headings: *a)* significant facts concerning reading interests and preferences; *b)* factors and conditions that influence reading interests. For the reading interests of adults see the section on the "sociology of reading."

Significant Facts Concerning
Reading Interests and Preferences

Summaries prepared by various investigators, such as Jordan (1: No. 198), Gray (1: 158-74), Gray and Munroe (6: No. 47), Celestine (7: No. 15). Friedman and Nemzek (14: No. 28), and Anderson (25: 217-71), have identified many facts concerning reading interests and preferences of which the following are highly significant.

1. Of large importance are the trends revealed by studies of the extent to which children read: *a)* The percentage of pupils who read books independently increases rapidly during the early, middle, and upper grades and remains relatively high on the average, but not uniformly so in different schools, during the secondary-school period. *b)* The average number of books read independently varies from ten to twenty in the sixth, seventh, and eighth grades. During the succeeding grades two distinct tendencies appear. In some schools a high average is maintained;

in other schools the number of books read on the average decreases notably. The latter trend is often attributed to distractions, to the increasing demands made by daily assignments on high-school pupils, and to the greater prominence of other interests.

2. Concerning newspapers and magazines the findings indicate that a large percentage of children above the third grade who have an opportunity to do so look at and read the former and, to a lesser extent, the latter. In the middle and upper grades the percentage of children who read newspapers and magazines regularly continues to increase. In some high schools studied, practically all pupils reported that they engaged regularly in newspaper or magazine reading or both. In other schools the findings were very disappointing. According to Levi (16: No. 72) the tenth grade ranks lowest at the secondary-school level in newspaper reading and in interest in current events. These findings, as well as those referred to in the preceding paragraph, indicate that the secondary school forms a critical period in respect to the reading habits of many young people. They show too that these schools face challenging reading problems which as yet have not been satisfactorily solved.

3. The results of published studies are in agreement concerning the general types of material preferred by children and young people. *a*) Pupils in both elementary and secondary schools read more fiction than any other type of material and like it better. When interest in juvenile fiction declines, pupils often fail to do additional reading because the home, the school, and the library fail to provide appropriate materials or to arouse new and compelling interests. *b*) Children and young people select for recreational reading a relatively small number of factual or informational books. Studies by Uhl (2: No. 63) and Smith (3: No. 46) show that pupils enjoy informational material that is simply and attractively written. As a result of the increasing attention given to the preparation of informational books for children, the amount of such reading has increased slowly but steadily during recent years. *c*) Pupils at all age levels with but rare exceptions prefer prose to poetry. Uhl found, however, that the reasons offered for not liking poetry usually attached to particular poems. Furthermore, some evidence has appeared

which supports the contention that the prevailing dislike for poetry among children is due in part to the poems they are asked to read and the methods of instruction used.

4. The outstanding fact about the reading preferences of children is that they differ widely at each grade and age level. Such differences can be readily explained by the fact that the interest of boys and girls differ to a greater or less extent with mental age, brightness, reading achievement, home environment, and previous experiences. It follows that a wide range of reading materials must be available at any grade level in order to provide adequately for the reading interests of all members of a group.

5. Although the reading interests of pupils differ widely at the respective grade levels, certain interests are more characteristic of pupils in some grades than in others. For example, Celestine (7: No. 15) found that children in the earliest grades were in general interested in animal stories, stories of children and familiar experience, nature stories of the fanciful type, and the simpler fairy tales. Between the ages of eight and ten animal stories of a realistic nature, stories of home and school life, of children in other lands, and of adventure, as expressed in the Boy Scout Series, become increasingly popular. During the period from ten to twelve Lazar (15: No. 49) found that the following elements made a general appeal: action, adventure, animal life and nature, child life, excitement, humor-mischief, thrills, mystery, realism, sportsmanship and bravery, suspense. Between twelve and fifteen broader interests are exhibited by boys and girls in their social and natural environment; history, biography, and adventure become increasingly interesting; books and articles on hobbies, how to make things, and specialized interests are read widely; furthermore, fiction of the sensational and mystery types is very popular. Such findings indicate that the interests of children change with increasing age and maturity. A more detailed analysis of published evidence shows that reading interests at any level merge gradually into those of another, varying with such factors as mental age, sex, background of experience, home influence, and availability of materials.

6. Comparisons of the reading interests of boys and girls reveal few significant differences in the primary grades. Between ten and thirteen years of age, however, striking differences

appear. Boys become increasingly interested in accounts of sports, adventure, war and scouting whereas girls become increasingly absorbed in stories of home and school life, fairy stories, and love stories. By the age of fifteen reading interests of both sexes are more or less definitely established. As indicated by the results of various studies, boys prefer newspapers and current events, accounts of sports, and materials relating to topics of special interest in the field of vocational activities. Girls express increasing preference for biography, books of humor, the all-fiction type of magazine, and poetry. In considering the interests of either boys or girls, those that are common to both sexes must be kept clearly in mind.

7. Comparisons of the reading interests of children of varying levels of intelligence reveal significant differences. Green (3: No. 25) found, for example, that pupils of low mental ability "preferred children as characters in their stories, read less current news, and less about specialized interests than those having medium or high intelligence." She also found more chronic readers of "series" books among the former. Terman and Lima (3: No. 49) reported that gifted children read more "science, history, biography, travel, folk tales, nature and animal stories, informational fiction, poetry, drama, and encyclopedias" and less "emotional fiction and stories of adventure and mystery." In a study extending over a number of years, Witty and Lehman (12: No. 108) found no evidence of a peak in reading interest at about fifteen years of age as reported in some schools. The data of these investigators indicated that gifted girls read more than gifted boys, but in the case of magazines and newspapers this relationship is reversed.

8. Throughout the last twenty-five years the results of studies of what pupils read independently have been disappointing when the quality and literary merit of the material are considered. This is true even in the case of college graduates. The attitude of investigators in general is well illustrated by the following conclusion of Persons (14: No. 62): "Does not the preponderance of fiction, the absence of reading that challenges the power to appraise and evaluate, the slight attention paid to poetry, the undiscriminating choice of magazines, the occupation with the tabloid newspaper" suggest a responsibility and offer a challenge to supervisors and teachers.

9. As a result of a study extending over a decade or more, Rasche (14: No. 68) reached the significant conclusion that the chief improvement made thus far in the reading interests of young people was among those who had learned to read with reasonable ease and understanding. He pointed out the urgent need of vigorous effort in the near future to improve the attainments of poor readers, to provide simple materials that relate to their interests, and to stimulate desirable motives for reading.

10. As a result of an elaborate survey among teachers and librarians, Rasche (4: No. 87) found that numerous methods of stimulating and directing reading interests have been developed and are in wide use both in the classroom and in the library. Through his efforts, as well as those of others, constructive suggestions are now available for all who are interested.

Factors and Conditions that Influence Reading Interests

Studies of reading interests and preferences have been supplemented by many investigations which throw light on the factors and conditions that promote or modify them. The results of these studies are very encouraging in that they show clearly that reading interests are influenced by many factors and conditions which the school or home can control.

1. Experiments carried on by Bamberger (1: No. 16) indicated clearly that the physical makeup of books influenced the choices of primary-grade pupils. In general books possessing the following characteristics were preferred: size—seven and one-half inches long by five inches wide by one inch thick; colors—blue, red, and yellow; many illustrations with crude and elementary colors, "having a high degree of saturation and a great deal of brightness"; pictures with storytelling qualities; wide margins, at least an inch in width. Some of these conclusions are tentative and require further experimentation for verification. The results suggest a type of consideration that is very important and that is receiving increasing attention.

2. Personal experience and experiments show clearly that teachers' preferences influence pupils' choices to a significant extent. In a study including seventy-three classes distributed from the third to the eighth grade inclusive, Wightman (1: No.

417) found that "the book the teacher most preferred and was enthusiastic over was pretty generally the one the class preferred." According to Wightman, the lesson taught by these findings "is that interest and inspiration are contagious and are essential if the great majority of public-school children ever form a love for reading."

3. In an experiment among seventh-grade pupils Green (1: No. 144) found that participation in developing standards for use in selecting books to read definitely influenced the choice of books read later. She attributed this to the fact that the training received developed standards which continued to function in the free choices of pupils. Although the evidence presented is not conclusive, it suggests the possibility of directing preferences through carefully planned training and guidance.

4. The comparative study of magazines has been found by Barnes (5: No. 8) to be helpful in providing critical knowledge of the relative merits of different types of magazines and in developing acceptable standards for the selection of periodical literature.

5. A free-reading program, as contrasted with a prescribed program, is according to LaBrant (14: No. 48) of great value in secondary schools in broadening the experiences and reading interests of pupils. This was particularly true when the guidance provided developed certain criteria relating to reading.

6. In a study made in Minneapolis by Cutright and Brueckner (6: No. 24), it was found that, all other things being equal, availability of books, as measured by distance of a school from a library, is a vital factor in promoting reading interests. This finding harmonizes with the results of studies of accessibility at more mature levels.

7. The foregoing study showed also that mere accessibility is no guarantee that pupils are interested in or engage in recreatory reading. "The necessity and importance of a constructive attack on the program in recreatory reading are emphasized by the results of this investigation" (6: No. 24, p. 137).

8. Various studies at both the elementary- and the secondary-school levels provide conclusive evidence that difficulty

of comprehension vitally affects the child's interest in what is read. Books that are within the pupil's grasp are discussed more freely, are completed in a larger percentage of cases, and serve more frequently as a point of departure for additional reading than is true if the material cannot be understood readily by the pupil.

9. As early as 1925 Jordan (3: No. 27) secured evidence which led him to conclude that the popularity of fiction was due in part "to the greater development and patronage of the moving picture." A year later Walter (4: No. 106) secured evidence that motion pictures aid materially in shaping the reading interests and tastes of girls. Subsequent studies confirm these early findings and show clearly that those who attend movies most usually read the larger number of books. In the judgment of some this is due to the fact that one who has broad interests will seek the companionship of books and go to the movies to satisfy them. There is much evidence, however, to support the view that movies help to arouse interests which are later satisfied through reading.

10. In a comparative study of the reading interests of high-school pupils in Illinois and Georgia, Punke (15: No. 61) found that the pupils who had radios in the home reported more leisure reading than did others. He found also that pupils in Illinois read more than those in Georgia. He attributed this difference largely to climatic conditions.

The studies to which reference has been made relate to some of the most important problems faced today in teaching reading. Because of the large place which reading holds in the life of most children, it is important that research continue in this field until far more is known concerning the reading interests and preferences of pupils and the factors and conditions that influence them. In addition continued experimentation is necessary in order to refine techniques now available and to develop new ones for stimulating and directing the reading interests of pupils representing different intelligence levels and home influences.

V. Reading Readiness

The Report of the National Committee on Reading (33) gave explicit recognition in 1925 to the fact that all pupils who enter the first grade are not equally well prepared for reading. It also emphasized the importance of training and experience that prepare for reading and identified, largely on the basis of experience, a series of requisites for beginning reading. Since the publication of this report numerous studies have been made of a series of issues relating to reading readiness. Some of the earliest of these studies emphasized the importance of better preparation for reading by calling attention to the surprisingly large percentage of nonpromotions at the end of the first grade due to failure to make satisfactory progress in reading.

The problem which has been studied most extensively relates to the factors which influence reading readiness. As early as 1925 Arthur (3: No. 2) studied the progress of 171 first-grade children and reached the conclusion that mental age is a very important factor in reading achievement. Studies by McLaughlin (6: No. 62) in Los Angeles and San Diego also supplied evidence that many of the first-grade pupils assigned to reading classes were mentally so immature that they were unable to learn to read successfully.

The results of such studies were soon supplemented by findings concerning the optimum mental age for beginning reading. As early as 1929 Raybold (7: No. 77) showed that pupils with a mental age of 76 months made more rapid progress in learning to read than those who were less mature. The investigator suggested, however, that further research was necessary to determine whether reading could be taught successfully to a less mature group. Two years later Morphett and Washburne (8: No. 74) compared the progress of first-grade pupils of different chronological and mental ages in vocabulary mastery, oral reading, and general reading progress and concluded that a mental age of 6.5 years is the optimum time at which to begin reading. They found, however, that some pupils between the mental ages of 6.0 and 6.5 years made satisfactory progress.

Investigators began early to identify other factors and conditions that influenced or were associated with progress in learning to read. For example, Risser and Elder (5: No. 77) MacLatchy (5: No. 50), and Teegarden (11: No. 81) found in general that pupils who received kindergarten training made more rapid progress in reading than those who did not. Teegarden found also that kindergarten-trained pupils had less tendency to reverse and confuse letters, due doubtless to practice in observation and in the discrimination of size and form. Other investigators directed attention to additional factors, such as physical fitness, emotional stability, conduct, and general ability to do first-grade work (5: No. 76); experiences relating to the themes to which the selections in beginning reading material relate (11: No. 92); ability to discriminate between letters and words (13: No. 19); and special training in language in the case of children with foreign-language handicaps (13: No. 35). In 1936 Harrison (13: No. 45) summarized both experimental evidence and expert opinion concerning the factors influencing reading readiness and outlined types of training and experience that prepare pupils for reading.

Paralleling the appearance of Harrison's report, Witty and Kopel (14: No. 92) prepared a critical survey of the scientific studies of reading readiness to determine the amount and character of the progress made in this field. As a result of this analysis they concluded that reading should be delayed "until children's background of experience and mental growth enable them to find meaning in the tasks presented to them; and until this process of maturation has engendered a condition in which reversals are few and perception of words and other meaningful units is possible." They implied that reading should be postponed for most children until they are about 8 or 9 years of age although they recognized that some "will turn spontaneously, joyfully, and successfully to reading in Grade I (or earlier)."

The pronouncement by Witty and Kopel has been preceded and followed by a series of intensive studies which aimed to determine with great accuracy the relation of various factors to success or failure in beginning reading. Gates and Bond (13: No. 39), for example, secured evidence that the relationship between some of the factors studied and progress in learning to read was by no means invariable. Their findings indicated also that reading readiness is not determined uniformly by the presence of certain attitudes or attainments but is the result of combinations of factors that differ somewhat in individual cases. Furthermore, the data secured showed that physiological handicaps, especially sensory, may interfere with progress in reading at any stage of development. The remedy in such cases lies, in part at least, in the "correction of the difficulties or adjustments to them rather than merely waiting for time to cure them."

In a subsequent study, Gates (14: No. 32) secured evidence which does not justify the postponement of reading until children are 8 or 9 years of age. By employing modern methods well adapted to individual differences, he found that reasonable progress in learning to read can be made by most first-grade pupils. He concluded, therefore, that "statements concerning the necessary mental age at which a pupil can be intrusted to learn to read are essentially meaningless." He does not deny that mental age is a factor in reading readiness nor does he oppose the plan "of attempting to determine the mental-age level or other characteristics of the pupil needed for making a successful beginning in reading." His findings emphasize the importance of studying these factors in relation to the nature of the program followed in teaching beginning reading.

Studies of the factors relating to reading readiness have been accompanied by various efforts to determine through objective tests a pupil's readiness for reading. As early as 1930 Deputy (8: No. 29) gave first-grade pupils a mental test, a visual-visual association test, a test of word selection, a visual-auditory association test, and a test of content comprehension and recall. Correlations between the test scores and reading achievement showed that the mental test provided the best single means of predicting reading achievement. The other tests, however, increased the predictive value of the mental test.

Stimulated by such findings as those of Deputy, a number of investigations have attempted to develop reading-readiness tests. For example, Lee, Clark, and Lee (11: No. 60) prepared a test which according to their data has a reliability coefficient of .97 and predicts scores on reading tests "better than two intelligence tests" and more accurately than did kindergarten teachers through the use of a scale of qualities designed for the purpose. Monroe (13: No. 62) also prepared a battery of reading-aptitude tests (visual, auditory, motor, articulation, language, and laterality) and presented evidence of their value in predicting success or failure in first-grade reading.

As tests of reading readiness developed, studies were made of their relative merits and of their value as compared with or used in conjunction with mental tests. After reviewing all the evidence available, Witty and Kopel (14: No. 92) concluded that, "when used in conjunction with an intelligence test and teachers' judgments of reading readiness in terms of health and physical and social maturity, these devices appear very helpful in determining when children should begin to receive reading instruction." These conclusions were supplemented helpfully by the findings of Senour (14: No. 70) who compared the value of the Detroit First-Grade Intelligence Test and the Metropolitan Reading Readiness Test. He found that either test may be used to advantage in predicting success in reading and that neither test has a distinct superiority over the other. Additional studies have been reported by Wright (14: No. 94), Grant (15: Nos. 30-31), Calvert (15: No. 9), Dean (16: No. 23), Huggett (16: No. 59) and Petty (16: No. 86). All of them support in general the conclusions of Witty and Kopel. Some of the evidence presented indicates that a well-conceived reading-readiness test has slightly greater predictive power than an intelligence test although the difference is slight. Whereas the results of studies of the relative merits of different reading-readiness tests indicate that some of them rank higher than others, final conclusions cannot be drawn until more extended studies have been made.

The fact was emphasized by certain investigators that reading-readiness tests differ in predictive value among schools and pupils. Petty (16: No. 86), for example, pointed out that such factors as home, social status, health, and disciplinary or personality problems might outweigh the influence of certain other factors that correlate highly in general with success in learning to read. Again, Gates, Bond, and Russell (16: No. 41) emphasized the fact that, to "the extent that the teacher's methods influence the pupil's techniques of learning, they also affect the predictive value of tests. Thus, if a teacher effectively emphasizes early phonetic attack, tests of blending, rhyming, etc., are likely to give higher correlations with reading progress in her class than in the class of a teacher who places less emphaisis on the phonetic approach." Thus, step by step, various facts and conditions that must be considered in determining the predictive value of reading-readiness tests are being identified.

A limited number of experiments have been reported which aimed to determine the effect on reading readiness of changes introduced into the school's program. Waters (11: No. 92) studied the types of experiences that pupils should have in order to read and understand the content of the readers used in the first grade. She then provided in the kindergarten types of experiences needed and found that an experimental group made far more rapid progress in reading during the first grade than did a control group. Peterson (14: No. 63) used the results of reading-readiness tests and other types of information in classifying first-grade pupils into "ready to read" and "transition" groups. The latter group was given special training which aimed to prepare them for reading. The rapid progress made in reading during the remainder of the year led Peterson to conclude that the orientation program had been very successful. Woods (15: No. 95) secured evidence of the value of so-called transition rooms in which training and experience that prepare for reading were provided. Although she admitted that the adoption of this plan had proved helpful to individual pupils, she felt that it obscured the real need which in her judgment was the postponement of reading. In the light of the facts presented earlier, her assumption may be seriously questioned.

The foregoing summary indicates that real progress has been made in securing an understanding of the factors and conditions that influence reading readiness and the types of measures that predict success in learning to read. With the facts now available it should be possible to carry on studies in the future that will be very productive in clarifying thinking concerning the requisites for learning to read, in developing tests that will reveal the extent of a pupil's readiness for reading, and in modifying teaching in the prereading period in order to promote desirable types of growth.

VI. Aims, Organization, and Time Allotment of Reading in the Grades

Although the aims of teaching reading have been discussed widely during recent years, the results of very few scientific studies of this problem have been published. The views that prevailed a quarter of a century ago are well represented by the results of the two studies. One of them (1: No. 136) shows the "most desirable results or outcomes of the teaching of reading in the elementary school" as reported by 715 teachers in a large city.

Aims	Per Cent of Teachers Reporting
Appreciation of good literature	68
Ability to comprehend	64
To secure information	40
Improvement in oral-reading ability	38
Enlargement of vocabulary	24
Mastery of the mechanics of reading	15
Training for leisure	15
Improvement in oral and written English	14
Improvement in study habits	10
Development of general mental qualities	7
Ability to reproduce and utilize materials read	6
Moral training	6
Use of books	1

A study (1: No. 314) by Reinoehl provided an analysis of the aims and content of reading instruction as given in 44 state courses of study for rural schools. The aims which appeared most frequently were not materially different from those listed above. However, such aims as "intelligent interpretation" and "power of discriminative reading" seemed to receive greater emphasis. In general, the aims that stood out most prominently in the two studies were "appreciation of good literature," "comprehension" and "intelligent interpretation," "effective oral reading," and a "mastery of the mechanics of reading." The results of such studies have serious limitations. They indicate primarily what teachers of reading and literature have emphasized in the past and what has appeared most frequently in courses of study. They summarize current practice rather than seek to determine the most valuable functions of reading in school or in social life.

The procedures involved in the latter type of study are illustrated in an investigation by Bobbitt (1: No. 33). He requested the teachers of literature to select from a comprehensive list those abilities "which should be kept in view as the goals of the work in literature and general reading." After the teachers had selected the abilities, a statement of objectives was drawn up and submitted to them for further consideration. An advantage of this procedure is that it is forward-looking and seeks to determine what the schools should aim at rather than what they are at present doing. A serious limitation of the procedure is that the aims selected are based solely on teacher judgment. The list is only as valid as the judgments of teachers are refined and exact.

During the last fifteen years the aims of teaching reading have been defined largely on the basis of analyses and the judgments of experts in the field. For example, the National Committee on Reading (33) adopted in 1925 the following objectives of instruction in reading: rich and varied experience through reading; strong motives for and permanent interests in reading; and desirable reading attitudes and economical and effective habits and skills. This analysis was continued by subsequent committees which presented their findings in 1936 (34) and in 1940 (25). The frequent preparation of such reports doubtless accounts in large measure for the absence of more objective studies since 1925.

Organization of the Curriculum in Reading

As the results of scientific studies of reading have become available, various efforts have been made to develop valid reading programs. The product of such efforts is exemplified in reports on reading in 1925 (33) and 1936 (34). The essential steps involved are: *a*) a critical survey and appraisal of the studies which throw light on the nature of reading, the general course of its development, and the factors that influence growth at each level of advancement; *b*) deliberate study to determine the implications of the findings as to the nature of the reading program; *c*) the organization of a reading program that harmonizes with pertinent facts about child development and growth in reading. The value of the resulting proposals depend in large measure upon the adequacy of the scientific evidence available and the efficiency with which it is analyzed and interpreted.

Without doubt the most elaborate effort (29) thus far to organize a reading program on the basis of scientific studies appeared in 1939. The results of scores of investigations relating to growth in attitudes and traits, to children's interests in reading, and to growth in specific phases of reading were studied with great care. The facts identified justified three general conclusions: first, pupils pass through various stages of development on their way to maturity in reading; second, the rate of progress varies widely among individuals; and, third, individual variations at a given grade level are due to the learner's general stage of development, his interest in reading, his attainments and difficulties in reading, his ability to learn, his nationality and background, and the amount and effectiveness of the stimulation and guidance that he receives. Further analysis of the results of available studies showed that a program of reading instruction could be organized to advantage in terms of five broad stages of development: *a*) the stage at which readiness for reading is attained; *b*) the initial stage in learning to read; *c*) the stage of rapid progress in fundamental reading attitudes and habits; *d*) the stage at which experience is extended rapidly through reading and increased power, efficiency, and excellence are attained; *e*) the stage at which reading interests, habits, and tastes are refined.

In presenting the foregoing statements, the fact is recognized that the validity of the stages mentioned has not been experimentally determined. They represent rather the judgment of individuals concerning the type of reading program that is justified by the results of scientific studies. Before these proposals can be finally accepted, further investigation is needed concerning the nature of reading, the course of its development, and the factors and conditions that influence progress. Furthermore, wide experimentation is needed to determine the best characterization of each stage of development, the teaching problems that are common to two or more of them, and the problems peculiar to each.

Time Allotment

For many decades more time was reserved on the daily schedule for reading than for any other subject. Arithmetic was its nearest competitor. A summary of available evidence in 1925 led to the following conclusions: "*a*) Schools in the large cities are giving more time to reading in each grade than are schools in the smaller cities or county schools. *b*) More time is given to reading in the first grade than in any other grade. *c*) The amount of time given to reading decreases more or less gradually from the first grade to the eighth grade. *d*) There are very wide differences among cities and within school systems as to the amount of time devoted to reading in any given grade. *e*) There is a distinct tendency to give less attention than formerly to arbitrary daily time allotments" (1: 34-35).

In commenting on the data presented in Table II the compiler stated that they "offer scant support to the statement often heard recently that less time is given to reading instruction now than was given a few years ago. Apparently for several years it has been customary to give 75 to 80 minutes a day to reading in grade I, gradually decreasing that amount to 30 or 35 minutes a day in grade VI." Since 1931 many school systems have definitely reduced the time allotted to reading; however, no data are available which summarize the situation within the last two or three years. The statement should be added that most of the studies reported thus far are more or less unsatisfactory because information concerning the number of minutes reserved for the reading period give very little insight concerning the total amount and character of the guidance given.

TABLE II

Average Time Allotments as Reported in Eight Different Investigations[1]

Investigator	Scope	Date	I	II	III	IV	V	VI	Average for All
Holmes	50 cities	1919	412	364	291	237	195	181	280
Kirk	31 schools	1923	325	250	250	125	125	125	200
Ayer	47 cities	1924	430	413	339	250	185	165	297
Latham	60 cities	1924	...	...	...	...	...	...	319
Bagley and Kyte	2600 teachers' programs	1926	454	377	305	244	197	180	292
Mann	444 cities	1926	388	348	293	212	168	149	260
Armentrout	33 schools	1927	346	317	298	219	156	141	246
Holman	157 schools	1931	379	331	270	224	185	181	262

[1](13: No. 3, p. 320)

VII. Nature, Content, and Grade Placement of Reading Materials

During the last two decades school curriculums have undergone radical reorganization. It would be natural to assume under these conditions that the nature and content of the materials used in teaching pupils to read would be carefully investigated. A survey of studies relating to reading shows that only a limited number of such investigations have been made. Those reported may be classified as follows: studies of the reading materials recommended in courses of study and those provided or actually used in school systems; studies of the content of readers; the vocabulary of readers; and the difficulty and grade placement of reading materials.

Studies of the Reading Materials Recommended or Used Most Frequently

A type of study which has been quite prominent in the past is concerned with the books and selections recommended most frequently in courses of study or provided or actually used in the schools. In 1913, for example, Bobbitt, Boyce, and Perkins (1: No. 34) examined 36 city and 14 state courses of study. The original tabulations included 138 authors and 296 titles. The findings were reported in two forms: *a)* an alphabetical list by authors showing the total number of times each book or selection was recommended, the grade for which it was recommended most frequently, and the range of grades represented; *b)* the second list included "the selections most frequently used in each grade, in the order of their frequency." Only selections mentioned nine or more times were included. The value of this type of study lies in the fact that it reveals to a greater or less extent the trend in practice at any given period. The findings are subject to all the criticisms that are inherent in the results of studies based on "frequency of practice."

Analyses of Required and Supplementary Reading Materials

A much more valuable type of study was made by Bobbitt (1: No. 32) as a part of the Indianapolis survey of reading. He collected copies of all the required and supplementary reading material in each elementary-school grade. An analysis was then made to determine the number of pages of required and supplementary reading in each grade. The findings indicated, first, a relatively small amount of required reading in the lower grades and a somewhat meager amount of supplementary material in the upper grades and, second, in some schools pupils "read about everything placed at their disposal while others cover but a minor fraction of it." Such findings have wide implications and provide a basis for numerous constructive recommendations.

The analysis was continued further, however, to determine the extent to which the reading materials provided experience in such fields as geography, history, industry, nature, science, health, and literature. He found, for example, that some of these fields were widely represented and that others were meagerly represented. He reported also that some of the books were "too difficult, abstract, and didactic" for the grades for which they were recommended; others were criticized as of value for fact learning but not for reading experience. Although such criticisms were largely subjective they suggested tentative standards which could be used in selecting appropriate reading materials for pupils at various levels of advancement.

Studies of the Content of Readers

A very illuminating study of the content of readers was reported by Robinson (8: No. 93) who analyzed and classified school readers published since prerevolutionary days into five periods on the basis of their major objectives. Before 1775 the objective was primarily religious; from 1775 to 1825 the religious and secular motives received about equal emphasis; from 1825 to 1875 the secular motives predominated; from 1875 to 1915 the literary ideal prevailed; since 1915 many objectives have dictated the content of readers. According to Smith (36) silent reading objectives determined the content of readers from 1915 to 1925 and since the latter date the recommendations of the National Committee on Reading have greatly influenced practice. The results of such studies justify the conclusion that the content of readers reflect to a surprising degree the changing interests, ideals, and aspirations of the nation as a whole.

A second type of study attempted to classify the content of readers under many different subjects or themes and to determine the amount of space given to each type at the respective grade levels. Starch (1: No. 354), for example, reported as early as 1921 the results of an analysis of the content of ten readers for each grade selected from twenty-four sets of readers. Sixteen types of content were chosen as the basis for classification, and the percentage of the content that belonged to each type was determined for each grade. The findings revealed notable differences between lower-grade and upper-grade readers. For example, the three leading classes in first-grade books related to "animals," "boys and girls," and "folklore." These together with poetry constituted over three fourths of all the materials included. On the other hand, the four chief classes of material in the eighth-grade books were "classics," "history and patriotism," "biography," and "poetry." The use of similar techniques has made it possible also to trace changes in the content of readers over a period of years. For example, Hockett (14: No. 43) compared the content of readers in current use in the primary grades with those used several years ago and found that "one of the greatest changes in the content of primary readers is the substitution of realistic stories and informational selections dealing with the common activities of children and adults for the fanciful folk tales and traditional nursery stories which received great emphasis fifteen years ago." A significant result of such studies has been a growing spirit of criticism not only of the types of material commonly included in readers but also of their interest appeal and value in enriching the experiences of the pupils taught.

A third type of study has sought to determine desirable and undesirable qualities of selections in readers. For example, Uhl (1: No. 389) submitted to teachers in 49 cities a list of preferred selections, based on the judgments of 3000 teachers. The list was accompanied with directions for critical comments concerning their characteristic qualities. Analyses were submitted by 741 teachers of the 15 best and the 15 poorest selections for use in their respective grades. As a check on teacher judgment tests based on certain selections were given to 529 pupils in grades 3 to 8 inclusive. Measures of both interest and comprehension were secured. Some of the important conclusions of the study follow: *a*) Much of the material in basal readers is unsatisfactory because it is too difficult, lacks action or plot; is unreal, depressing, monotonous; is not well told; and is "too long or scrappy." *b*) Many of the selections meet with almost universal approval because of their interest appeal, dramatic action, and valuable content. *c*) Newer types of informational material prove very successful and provide "content which has ample social justification." Such studies particularly when the responses and judgments of pupils are included, provide a valuable body of information for the use of authors and publishers of readers as well as those responsible for their selection and use in schools.

Studies of the Difficulty and Grade Placement of Reading Material

As an aid in determining the difficulty and probable grade placement of reading materials, various techniques have been developed which differ materially in the amount of time involved and the number of elements considered. One of the simplest procedures was developed by Johnson (7: No. 50) who used the percentage of polysyllabic words as a measure of difficulty. A second method was developed by Lewerenz (6: No. 58) who found after experimentation that a valuable measure of difficulty was the percentage of words beginning with *w, h, b, i,* or *e*. A much more detailed method was developed by Vogel and Washburne (5: No. 94) who made a study of the vocabulary difficulty, sentence structure, parts of speech, paragraph construction, and physical make-up of 152 books chosen from the "Winnetka Graded Book List." After the elements had been tabulated, those which showed most definite change from grade to grade were chosen for further study. As a result of various statistical studies it was found that the following elements had the greatest predictive value: "Number of different words occurring in a sampling of 1000 words," "number of prepositions (including duplicates) occurring in a 1000-word sampling," "number of different words (including duplicates) in a 1000-word sampling not occurring in Thorndike's list," and "number of simple sentences in 75 sample sentences." The data secured through such counts were later incorporated into a formula which provided a single index of difficulty. The method was revised by Washburne and Morphett (15: No. 90) in order to effect needed improvements. After extended experimentation to determine a satisfactory procedure in selecting readers and other books for children, Washburne and Morphett maintained that two types of information are essential: first, the judgment of expert children's librarians concerning such factors as interest appeal, content, and literary style and, second, the results of statistical studies of the materials to determine grade placement.

VIII. Methods of Teaching

During the last three decades keen interest has been expressed in improved methods of teaching reading. The studies reported in this field are so numerous that an adequate summary and critical evaluation would require more space than has been allotted in this volume to the entire report on reading. It will be possible, therefore, to summarize briefly only some of the more significant results of research relating to methods of teaching reading.

A Modern Systematic Method *versus* Other Procedures

Although reading has usually been taught through the use of a carefully planned systematic procedure, a number of educators of high repute maintain that essential attitudes and habits can be established equally well, if not more effectively, in other ways. For example, Meriam (7: No. 59) contends that: *a)* "The best way to teach reading is not to teach reading, but to provide the occasion...in which certain reading functions.... *b)* Let pupils read to learn; incidentally they will learn to read." In support of his contention Meriam presented data which show that a group taught in harmony with the foregoing principles did better than public-school children who received systematic training in reading. Unfortunately the comparability of the groups was not considered, and the experiment was very loosely controlled in other respects.

Many educators who favor a highly integrated activity curriculum in the primary grades also favor the use of incidental procedures in teaching pupils to read. They present data which indicate that those who follow such programs do about as well as those who receive systematic training in reading. Unfortunately most of these studies were loosely controlled and failed to secure adequate measures of progress in reading and in related phases of the curriculum. Lee (10: No. 50), on the other hand, secured evidence that activity schools in California were retarded in reading in the first grade from one to seven months as compared with other schools. Two questions raised by the investigator were: "Do most activity programs provide an enriching experience in vocabulary which is of more ultimate value than is the usual instruction in reading?" "Does the postponement of the teaching of reading increase or decrease the number of poor readers?" Obviously the need is urgent for further experimental study of some of the basic problems suggested by these questions.

A far more productive type of study was made by Gates, Batchelder, and Betzner (3: No. 17) who studied the relative merits of a "modern systematic method" of teaching and an "opportunistic method." Twenty-five pairs of first-grade pupils were used in the experiment. Through the use of preliminary and final tests, the progress of the pupils was determined in reading, spelling, numbers, drawing, information gained, and social, emotional, moral, and other attitudes and habits. In respect to average achievement in oral and silent reading, the group taught by the "modern systematic method" was distinctly superior but other evidence indicated that the "opportunistic method" was advantageous in respect to the development of interest, initiative, determination, and other personal and social traits. It appears, therefore, that some systematic instruction in beginning reading supplemented by wide reading in other school activities may be the most effective procedure to follow.

The general problem with which we are here concerned has been studied from a somewhat different point of view in the more advanced grades. For example, Zirbes, Keelor, and Miner (2: No. 73) studied the relative merits of intensive instruction in reading as contrasted with independent silent reading in the second grade. The results showed that the average growth in reading ability was about the same for each group. However, the brighter pupils profited more from independent silent reading and the slower pupils from intensive instruction. Similar results were secured by O'Brien (8: No. 76) in the fifth and sixth grades, who concluded that normal and bright children require only a minimum of "mechanical and remedial instruction" and that interest and wide reading cannot be depended upon to increase the reading abilities of slow learners.

The results of these and other studies justify two important conclusions: first, that each of the general procedures involved in the experiments was of much greater value for some purposes than for others and, second, that systematic training in reading, supplemented by wide reading in other school activities and by free reading in the library, is essential to meet the needs of all pupils. The studies show also that the desirable amount of systematic instruction in reading varies with the interests, needs, and capacities of the pupils.

Relative Merits of Different Systematic Methods of Teaching Reading

Three types of studies have been made of the relative merits of various methods of teaching beginning reading: measures of the achievement of pupils taught by different methods; experiments to determine the relative merits of specific methods; and analyses of the progress and difficulties of pupils taught by different methods. The results of such studies do not supply convincing evidence of the superiority of some methods and the inferiority of others. One fact that stands out clearly, however, is that a given method does not always secure equally satisfactory results. The evidence available supports the belief that factors other than the specific method used, such as the skill of the teacher, the economic level of the pupils, their nationality, and their capacity to learn, influence progress in reading to a surprising extent.

A second conclusion justified by experimentation is that contrasting methods emphasize different aspects of reading. This fact is brought out clearly in a study by Buswell (1: No. 53) who followed for a year the progress of pupils taught by different methods—the one, an elaborate phonetic method which emphasized word recognition; the other, a method which emphasized a correct reading attitude and meaningful experiences. A detailed analysis of test results, eye-movement records, and observations made at intervals of six weeks throughout the year showed that the first method promoted ability to follow the lines and to pronounce all the words, but no vital concern for the content. A significant outcome of the second method was keen interest in the content but slow progress in word recognition and in ability to follow the lines. Buswell concluded that sooner or later pupils must make progress in all of the aspects of reading represented by the two methods.

A third conclusion justified by the experiments in this field is that certain methods are more effective with given types of pupils than with others. Bond (12: No. 6), for example, pointed out the fact that pupils with auditory deficiencies do not profit most from a method which emphasizes the sound values of words. Similarly pupils who are visually handicapped may not respond well to a method which requires close visual discriminations. Averill and Mueller (2: No. 2) presented evidence showing that the same methods are often not equally effective with pupils of different intelligence levels. The need is urgent, as it was a decade ago, for analytical studies and experiments which aim to determine the elements of strength and weakness in each method now used widely in classrooms, the conditions under which it proves most effective, and the types of pupils for which it is best adapted.

Value or Effect of the Use of Specific Methods and Procedures

Cutright (13: No. 18) reviewed evidence concerning manuscript writing *versus* cursive or script writing and found that its use in the first grade is a distinct aid to pupils in learning to read. Haefner (14: No. 40) summarized the results of studies relating to the use of the typewriter and concluded: "While the volume of experimental evidence is still somewhat limited, it may be safely concluded that the typewriter influences elementary-school reading in a positive manner and to an important degree."

Wide interest has been expressed recently in the use of such supplementary aids as games (15: No. 29) in recognizing words (for example, Read-O), workbooks (8: No. 41), and other practice materials (11: No. 70). The evidence, in general, is favorable to the use of a moderate amount of material of these kinds. They often aid in establishing basic reading attitudes and habits. The statement should be added that they are most helpful, as a rule, in the case of pupils who make slow progress in learning to read. Additional studies are needed to determine the types of growth that each promotes and the conditions under which it can be used most effectively.

The use of slides in presenting first-grade reading materials was studied by Jardine (16: No. 61) and found to be valuable, particularly among the slower pupils. The fact that the materials presented on slides coud be readily adapted to the needs of the pupils added greatly to their value. Lee (16: No. 71) used the metronoscope with classes in various grades for a portion of the reading period throughout a year. He reported that, as a result, the number of first-grade retentions had been notably reduced and the general achievement in reading greatly improved throughout the school.

Methods of Promoting Growth in Word Recognition

Hamilton (1: No. 155), Judd (1: No. 204), and others early established the fact that, as a rule, the general characteristics of a word are the clues by which it is recognized. When the words are strange or difficult, however, additional distinctions within the word are necessary. As pointed out by Judd, "unless the school trains the pupil to work out his words systematically, he will do it badly and will exhibit confusion." By 1925 (1: No. 67) the following aids to word recognition had been identified: the context, the total configuration of a word, significant details of words; phonetic analysis; the principles of syllabication and accent; and the use of the dictionary. Within recent years various experiments have been reported which show that training in ability to recognize significant details of words, to master letter form and sound, to see likenesses and differences in words, and to identify familiar words in new words are valuable aids in promoting accuracy and independence in word recognition.

The chief controversy in this field relates to the value of phonetics as an aid in teaching pupils to read. For decades, phonetics was emphasized more vigorously than any other aid to word recognition. One advantage of its use is that it helps pupils in the recognition of many words known orally but which are unfamiliar in printed form. Some of the disadvantages of vigorous emphasis on phonetic analysis are that it directs attention chiefly to the form and sound of words rather than to their meaning; furthermore, when applied to unphonetic words, the results are often disastrous. The data secured in a score of experimental studies, particularly those by Gates and Russell (16: No. 43) and Agnew (16: No. 1), justify the conclusion that a moderate amount of training in phonetic analysis is valuable for most pupils. Evidence presented in some of the reports indicates that the most valuable results are secured if the amount of emphasis on phonetics is limited in the first-grade and the training continued in the second and third grade until all the important elements have been learned.

Methods of Improving Meaning Vocabularies

During recent years problems relating to the expansion of the meaning vocabularies of pupils have assumed large importance. This is due to two facts: first, the results of vocabulary studies provide striking evidence of the large vocabulary burden in readers, in juvenile literature, and in textbooks in various fields; and, second, the findings of Hilliard (1: No. 170) and others show that, of the factors influencing comprehension, extent of meaning vocabulary ranks next to intelligence in importance. Stimulated by these facts, Gray and Holmes (15: No. 35) made an extensive survey of the various methods in current use for extending and enriching meaning vocabularies and carried on a series of investigations to determine the relative merits of the incidental and direct method of promoting vocabulary growth.

The survey of literature revealed the fact that many methods are now used both in elementary and high schools. Among them are the "natural" or incidental method, specific study of words in context, casual emphasis on new words at the beginning of a class period, direct teaching of meanings, drill on lists of words, and use of dictionaries and other sources of help. Evidence of the value of each of these methods was found. The conclusion was reached that a broad program of training should include various types of guidance. It seemed clear also that more or less specific emphasis upon meanings, supplemented by help derived from the context, would prove valuable in study activities. When the relative merits of the direct and incidental methods were studied experimentally in the case of fourth-grade history classes, it was found that specific guidance in securing the meaning of new words resulted not only in more rapid growth in meaning vocabulary but also in comprehension in silent reading, in accuracy in oral reading, and in ability to express oneself fluently and accurately about the topics discussed. Such findings have already stimulated widespread interest in classroom studies to determine procedures which are most effective in increasing meaning vocabularies in various subjects and at different grade levels.

Methods of Improving Comprehension

For at least three decades teachers and specialists in reading have engaged regularly in studies to determine ways in which the comprehension of what is read may be improved. By 1925 (1: 104-12), the following conditions and procedures had been found to be effective: a clear recognition by teachers of improvement in comprehension as an objective of teaching reading; wide reading for specific purposes; a knowledge of the results of practice in reading to comprehend; silent-reading lessons based on experience; doing individual seatwork through the use of written or printed directions; engaging in silent reading with attention directed to meanings; adapting guidance in silent reading to group and individual needs; emphasis on the elements on which meaning depends, such as topic sentences, relational words, effect of different types of modifying words, phrases, and clauses; practice in silent-reading exercises; increasing meaning vocabulary, selecting central thoughts of paragraphs and organizing them in logical sequence, and retaining and reproducing the important points read; developing motives for improvement, securing favorable conditions for practice, diagnosing and removing hindrances, and securing persistence in effort; self-analysis and study of the psychology of reading.

Since 1925 numerous supplementary procedures have been tried out experimentally: training in organization, retention, and vocabulary building, by Alderman (2: No. 1); reading with a specific problem in mind when definite information is wanted, by Distad (4: No. 24); the use of an outline in reading, by Wright (7: No. 105); reading guided by questions *versus* reading and rereading, by Holmes (8: No. 54); and reading to determine what sentences say, to select a few words that give the main thought, and to select the most essential sentences, by Yoakam and Truby (3: No. 56). These and other types of studies have been very productive in securing a clearer understanding of various procedures which may be used in increasing comprehension. Thus far very little has been done to determine the patterns of guidance that are most effective in reading for different purposes.

Methods of Increasing Speed of Reading

Early studies relating to speed of reading led in three important conclusions (1: 147): *a*) speed may be increased through appropriate methods at various levels of school progress; *b*) notable increases in speed may often be made without impairing comprehension; *c*) the effect of speed drills on comprehension varies with the emphasis which is placed on both speed and comprehension in the training exercises. These studies showed also that the following methods and procedures are effective in increasing the speed of reading: speed drills on short passages; short-exposure exercises supplemented by speed drills; training in rapid reading, training to reduce vocalization, and training to increase span of recognition; increasing the amount of reading done; pacing eye movements; developing motive for improvement, securing favorable conditions for practice, studying the factors of success, and securing persistence in practice.

During the last fifteen years experimentation has been continued in this field with very valuable results. For example, Good (4: No. 38) found that speed of reading may be influenced through encouragement or discouragement and by the request to skim or to reproduce. Scott (3: No. 44) secured evidence that drill in the rapid recognition of isolated phrases does not materially affect fluent recognition of meaningful material. Thus step by step a clearer understanding of desirable steps in increasing speed of reading has been attained. Three problems which are in urgent need of further study relate to the relative merits of different methods in increasing speed, the types of training that are most effective for different kinds of readers at the respective grade levels, and the most effective distribution of practice to secure permanent improvement.

IX. Reading in the Content Fields

Wide interest in reading problems in the content fields was stimulated about two decades ago through studies of the correlation between reading achievement and scholastic attainments. A summary (1: 21) of the early studies in this field showed that: *a)* there is a fair degree of positive relationship, varying from .25 to .60, between reading achievement and class marks; *b)* this relationship varies with the reading tests used, the subjects involved, and the school studied; *c)* factors other than intelligent reading, such as the purpose and determination of the pupil, influence success in schoolwork. These findings have been supplemented recently by the results of an extended study by Bond (16: No. 13) who found that "varying degrees of relationship exist between the several aspects of ability in reading and composite ninth-grade achievement." Her data showed also that slow readers are at an advantage in composite achievement. Furthermore, rapid reading is "a definite help in enlarging vocabulary and broadening literary acquaintance" whereas slow reading "is characteristic of high achievement in science, mathematics, and Latin." Obviously then "varying degrees of relationship exist between the several aspects of reading and each of the various ninth-grade subjects."

As the general relationship between reading achievement and school attainments was recognized, pertinent lines of inquiry were started by different groups of investigators. One such series of studies related to the relative merits of different study procedures in "work-type" reading. The work of Good (3: No. 19) is typical of this series. He carried on studies at the high-school and college levels to determine the relative merits of extensive and intensive reading in the social sciences as measured by *a*) range and accuracy of information, *b*) ability in problem solving of ability to apply knowledge to given situations, *c*) ability to see relationships or to outline, *d*) ability to reproduce ideas or thought units, and *e*) ability to retain material read. Good (3: No. 21) also studied the effect of a single reading of a given body of material as compared with the effect of two readings of the same material. The tests given in the first of these experiments showed that in general extensive reading resulted in better achievement than intensive reading. The fact was pointed out, however, that each type of reading had certain advantages. In the case of outlining and in solving certain problem situations, extensive reading was superior. In the reproduction of ideas, intensive reading ranked higher. In regard to retention, extensive reading was superior as measured by information and problem retests, but less effective as measured by reproduction retests.

In the second experiment Good found that two readings at a normal rate "prove definitely more effective in terms of the information-test scores than one reading at normal rate." Good took the position that since one reading resulted in a fair mastery of the passages read, it would be much better to read a new selection relating to the same topic than to spend the same amount of time in rereading. This view is tenable, of course, only as long as the reader's purpose remains the same. The investigations by Good were preceded by those of Germane (1: Nos. 110-114) who studied experimentally such problems as "the value of a controlled mental summary as a method of studying," "outlining and summarizing compared with rereading," and "the value of the corrected summary as compared with rereading." As a result of the work of Germane, Good, and other investigators a body of information has developed concerning the merits of certain reading and study procedures that are generally applicable.

Paralleling investigations relating to general study procedures, questions arose concerning the advisability of specific training in reading in different subject fields. One type of evidence supporting such training was secured by Stevens (9: No. 99) who found that achievement in problem reading is more closely correlated with achievement in problem solving than is achievement in general reading or in fundamental operations. Such findings emphasize the importance of training in the kinds of reading and thinking required in a given course. Additional evidence of the value of training in reading in specific subjects was secured by Jacobson (9: No. 53) in an experiment to improve the achievement of ninth-grade pupils in reading in general science. The exercises provided were concentrated on three major aspects of reading and study; namely, comprehension, organization, and location of material.

Comparisons of the progress of the experimental and control groups led to the following conclusion: "*a*) Reading lessons given in general science produce superior knowledge of general science to an extent which cannot be explained by chance. *b*) Reading lessons given in general science have a beneficial effect on the general scholastic achievement of ninth-grade pupils. *c*) Reading lessons of the type used in this experiment are more beneficial to poor initial readers than to good initial readers." It may be inferred from the last conclusion that the training given related to the more rudimentary phases of the problems studied. If more advanced training had been given, it is fair to assume that superior students would have profited also. This assumption finds support in the conclusions of Woodring and Flemming (13: No. 95) who summarized in the following terms recent trends in the improvement of study; "the high school must face a twofold responsibility of providing corrective instruction in reading skills for the pupils who have not developed essential abilities in the elementary grades for the understanding and organization of printed materials; and of developing during the high-school experience fundamental skills upon new and higher levels."

In the light of the foregoing findings and conclusions the types of reading activities required in different curriculum fields assume large importance. One of the early studies in this field was made by Monroe (1: No. 266) who secured the cooperation of 317 teachers in the seventh and eighth grades and in the high school in an effort to identify the types of learning in textbook study "in which reading is the central activity." Twelve types of learning were selected for further study: "comprehension of material read plus memorization so that it can be reproduced"; "preparation of a summary which contains the central ideas of the assignment studied"; "preparation of an outline which gives the principal points and supporting details arranged to show order of relative importance and relations to each other"; "obtaining information for the purpose of solving problems, or answering questions"; "extension of one's range of general information by reading widely material directly related to a given subject"; "discovery of collateral or illustrative material for topics or problems under discussion"; "enlargement of vocabulary"; "appreciation of the significance of each word used in a concisely expressed statement of principle"; "a clear comprehension of the essential conditions of a problem which is to be solved"; "discovery of new or supplementary problems relating to the topic being studied"; "drawing valid conclusions from given data or statements"; "following directions with accuracy and reasonable speed."

A much more recent study of a similar type was made by McAllister (14: No. 51) who analyzed the content of the syllabi of courses required of freshmen in junior colleges to determine different ways in which reading might be used in studying them. The activities were organized under the following headings: "reading for pleasure and recreation"; " ascertaining the purpose of reading before beginning to study"; "rapid reading or skimming"; "assimilating and retaining information"; "amplifying understanding of a topic or problem"; "interpreting and executing directions"; "proofreading written reports"; "apprehending relationships"; "comparing and contrasting"; "organizing information"; "evaluating reading material"; "drawing inferences from reading." In both this study and the one by Monroe the extent to which each of the reading activities listed functioned in the different school subjects or fields was determined. The impressive facts revealed were that reading is used for many different purposes in each subject and that the reading activities in one subject differ significantly from those in another.

As the general nature of the reading problem in each content field became better understood, intensive studies were made to determine the nature of the specific difficulties in reading which pupils encounter in each field. One fact which stands out impressively in practially all such studies relates to the need for a wider meaning vocabulary on the part of most pupils. A closely related deficiency was identified by Dewey (13: No. 20) who made a study of reading comprehension difficulties in American history. He found that "children in the eighth grade do not seem to possess sufficient backgrounds in the fields of history, civics, economics, or geography, or even in general experience, to understand and interpret such selections as were used in this investigation. These limitations of training and experience should be clearly recognized in presenting such highly technical material as judicial decisions, problems of Federal finance, government theory, or economic processes." Such findings indicate that the problem of developing good reading habits involves far more than training in habits and skills.

Additional difficulties were identified by McAllister (8: No. 66) in a study of the reading of seventh- and eighth-grade pupils in American history, mathematics, and general science. Fifty difficulties were identified which were classified under the following headings: those growing out of the pupils' method of attack; those caused by inability to recognize relationships; those arising from lack of knowledge of subject matter; those caused by inaccuracies; and those caused from lack of clearness in the directions given to children. In a subsequent study (8: No. 67) he found that needed guidance could be given with distinct advantage to the pupils in connection with regular study activities of the course. "Such guidance may take the form of group instruction or, in extreme cases, of individual training." It "not only assists pupils with the regular work of a course but also stimulates independent effort and self-confidence."

One of the most promising results of such findings and recommendations is the wide interest which has been exhibited recently by both teachers and investigators in the improvement of reading in various school subjects. There is scarcely a subject or level of advancement from the primary grades to the university in which productive studies have not been reported. The next steps should be a deliberate survey by those interested in each content subject of the progress which has been made in the scientific study of reading problems and the development of an adequate research program in each field. The progress made in this connection by leaders in the Romance Languages is noteworthy.

X. Diagnosis and Remedial Teaching

The term "remedial reading," as used widely today, refers to constructive work with pupils who encounter more or less difficulty in reading. In the case of pupils who are not greatly retarded or handicapped, corrective work is provided largely through group instruction, supplemented by more or less individual help. In the case of the pupils who are seriously disabled in reading, clinical procedures are adopted in respect both to diagnosis and to remediation. Inasmuch as there is no sharp line of differentiation between these two types, they will be considered together.

As a result of a survey of recent literature in this field, Traxler (16: No. 112) identified six specific aspects of the problem to which the research done thus far relates: *a*) the "objectives" of diagnosis and remediation; *b*) "identification of retarded readers"; *c*) the "diagnosis" of difficulties (including causal factors); *d*) "organization of instructional groups"; *e*) "remedial training"; *f*) "evaluation of progress." This outline is so inclusive that it will be used as the basis for the brief discussion that follows.

Very little has been done directly through research to define the objectives of diagnosis and of corrective and remedial work in reading. The motives for such activities have arisen from the fact that a surprisingly large percentage of boys and girls are more or less seriously handicapped in activities that involve reading. Not infrequently from 20 to 25 per cent of the pupils of a class encounter serious difficulty in doing required reading (34: 121). Such findings have stimulated effort throughout the nation to identify poor readers and to provide for them the types of group or individual help needed. As pointed out by Traxler it is not practicable to try "to establish a general set of objectives that can be adopted in all remedial programs since the purposes are largely dependent on the deficiencies and the needs of the individual pupil...." He mentioned, however, the following objectives as common to nearly all published lists: "*a*) the establishment of effective basic reading habits; *b*) the promotion of permanent interests in and habits of independent reading; *c*) the development of skills in work-type reading; *d*) the fostering of desirable reading attitudes; *e*) the deepening of appreciations for literary, scientific, and other types of writing; *f*) acquaintance with and facility in library skills; *g*) the widening of the conceptual background of the pupils; and *h*) the improvement of the methods of thinking employed by the pupils while reading and the formation of habits of thoughtful, critical, analytical reading" (16: No. 112, p. 4).

Two methods of identifying poor readers have been employed widely; namely, observation and the use of tests. The first method has distinct practical value but very little scientific value as it is commonly employed in classrooms today. The second method is far more objective and provides types of data of large significance in identifying poor readers and their needs. Research agencies have been very energetic of late in determining both the validity and the reliability of the tests used in diagnosis. For example, most comprehension tests that are given widely today have a reliability of .90 or more. Unfortunately, most tests of speed of reading are too short to be very reliable. This difficulty can be overcome by using two or more tests of speed. Available evidence shows also that, whereas the norms on diagnostic tests are often questionable, the results of the tests indicate the relative rank of pupils with high reliability. Two recent reports (25: Chs. 9, 10; 37: Chs. 5, 7) summarize at length the various studies that have been made of instruments of diagnosis and discuss their relative merits for use both in groups and with individuals.

After poor readers have been identified, their diagnosis is continued to determine more accurately the nature of their reading deficiency and to identify the causal factors involved. In this connection notable progress has been made during recent years in the development of tests which provide measures of attainments and needs in various aspects of reading. Such tests as the Monroe Diagnostic Battery make possible very detailed studies of the nature of the pupil's deficiencies in basic habits of recognition. Furthermore eye-movement records (1: No. 53) indicate clearly the extent to which mature habits have been acquired and the nature of some of the difficulties which the reader encounters. The need is urgent for the development of additional diagnostic batteries for use by teachers in the upper grades, high school, and college in analyzing the nature of the pupil's deficiencies in reading.

Diagnosis involves also the identification of the causal factors that operate in a given case. As a result of the critical analysis of research findings, Monroe and Bachus (14: No. 58) classified the causative factors that contribute to reading disability into five areas: *a*) constitutional factors, including visual and auditory defects, difficulties in motor control, physical defects, and debilitating conditions; *b*) "intellectual factors," including general intelligence, "verbal disabilities," and "peculiarities in modes of thought"; *c*) "emotional factors," including (i) those "which are primary in causing reading disabilities" such as "general emotional immaturity," "excessive timidity," "predilection against reading" and "all school activities," (ii) those "which are the result of reading disability" and "in turn retard the child's progress," and (iii) those which occur "when reading becomes linked in the child's mind with some unpleasant or emotional experience"; *d*) "educational factors," including deficiencies in reading readiness, poor adjustment of materials and methods to the pupil's needs, lack of interest or motivation, and inadequate provision for pupils who are deficient in reading; *e*) "environmental factors." A recent summary and series of original studies by Bennett (16: No. 6) show clearly that most of these factors operate to a greater or less extent in individual cases.

In order to identify the factors and conditions that contribute to reading deficiency in individual cases various tests and procedures are now used widely. They include: *a*) mental tests to determine the mental age, intelligence quotient, and certain mental traits, such as power of association; *b*) visual tests, such as the Keystone Ophthalmic Telebinocular Tests and the Ophthalmograph; *c*) auditory tests, such as the 4A audiometer; *d*) personality tests such as the Bernreuter Inventory; *e*) interest inventories and school-history blanks. Furthermore, the efforts of the school diagnostician are often supplemented by members of the medical profession, ophthalmologists, optometrists, psychiatrists, visiting teachers, and social case workers. Every means possible is being employed by many investigators in this field to secure as complete and detailed body of evidence as possible on which to base conclusions.

As the nature of a reader's deficiency and the causal factors involved are understood, problems relating to the administration of instruction arise. As a result of a survey of published studies, Traxler (16: No. 112) concluded that two general types of group organization have been employed: "the formation of regular classes in which part or all the time is devoted to remedial reading" and "the setting-up of small groups of pupils with similar difficulties for instruction at free periods." In the case of seriously retarded pupils or those with specialized deficiencies, instruction has been individual. Further analysis showed that various plans are used in instructing regularly scheduled classes: "*a*) a short intensive period of instruction using perhaps six weeks during the school year, *b*) the alternating of periods of reading and regular subject matter, offering first a reading unit, then a unit of the regular course, then another reading unit, etc., *c*) the continuous teaching of reading one period a day throughout an entire semester or even a whole year *d*) utilization of the content of the regular course as the basis of the remedial reading" (16: No. 112, p. 13). The results of studies in which these various plans of organization have been used indicate that all of them are more or less effective. No objective evidence is available concerning their relative advantages and disadvantages. In the case of seriously retarded pupils the evidence available is distinctly favorable to individual instruction.

The chief decision that must be reached in planning remedial teaching for a group or individual relates to the type or types of instruction that are most appropriate. This must be determined, of course, in terms of the nature of the pupils' deficiencies. Some of the types of activities reported in remedial studies follow (16: No. 112): "free reading following lines of interest with a minimum of supervision"; "training the basic skills of work-type reading"; carefully planned exercises aimed at overcoming specific difficulties; "training in both general and technical vocabulary"; and "practice in improving methods of thinking while reading." These and many other procedures have been used to distinct advantage. In fact, scarcely a method has been reported thus far that has not produced improvements. As pointed out by Dearborn, Buswell, and others, virtue may not lie so much in the specific methods used as in the stimulation and leadership of the teacher, the determination of the pupil to succeed, or some other like factor. The need is urgent for studies of the merits of different procedures now in use and of the purposes for which they can be employed to greatest advantage.

The general teaching procedures referred to above have been supplemented by a series of specialized remedial techniques which have excited wide attention. Among them are the kinaesthetic method of promoting word recognition; the use of the flash meter in developing greater accuracy in perceiving words; the use of the metronoscope and films in presenting reading material under controlled conditions of word spacing and time in order to stimulate right directional movements of the eyes in reading, to increase the span of recognition, and to increase speed of reading. Evidence has already been secured of the value of each of these devices. Their superiority to other methods of achieving the same ends has not been experimentally established.

As indicated in the preceding paragraphs, the value of diagnosis and remediation has been objectively established. Three urgent problems which are faced today relate to: *a*) the need for the cooperation of all agencies that can contribute to an understanding of the nature of reading deficiencies and of the causative factors involved; *b*) wide experimentation to refine the techniques of diagnosis and remediation; *c*) the careful study of the deficiencies and needs of pupils in regular classes to reduce to a minimum the number who require remedial treatment.

XI. Hygiene of Reading

Problems relating to the hygiene of reading have commanded the attention of investigators for more than fifty years. Among the problems studied are those relating to style of type, legibility of different letters, length of line, regularity in length of line, distance between the lines (leading), size of type, thickness of the vertical strokes of letters, spacing of words and letters and the space between the vertical strokes of letters, color of type, color and texture of paper, color of pictures, and size of the book. Of these problems those relating to size of type, legibility of different letters, length of line, and color of paper have been studied most intensively.

Results of Earlier Studies

In 1925 a critical summary (1: 191-203) of studies relating to the hygienic requirements of printed materials was prepared which led to the following conclusions: "For purposes of legibility, reading material should be printed in black on white glossless paper in a plain style of type. The lines should be about ninety millimeters in length." Some evidence was presented which indicated that a slightly longer line could be used without reducing the reader's efficiency. The fact was emphasized that "the left-hand margin should be regular, except for paragraph indentations." No conclusive evidence was found concerning the character of the right-hand margin. Leading was found to be important although the most appropriate amounts for different sizes of type had not been determined. Some of the investigators, such as Huey and Shaw, believed that leading could be sacrificed, if necessary, for larger type.

As implied by the foregoing statement, size of type was recognized as one of the most important factors determining legibility. Its significance was emphasized by the findings of Griffing and Franz (1: No. 149) who found that fatigue increased rapidly as the size of the type decreased. On the other hand, eye-movement studies by Judd (1: No. 204) and by Gilliland (1: No. 120) showed that in the case of mature readers rate of reading and eye-movement habits are little affected when the type is varied in size within fairly wide limits. Nevertheless, investigators favored somewhat universally the use of relatively large type for the first four grades. All the evidence available indicated that Shaw's recommendations (1: No. 337) concerning the heights and leadings could be followed safely: first grade, 2.6 mm (width of leading, 4.5 mm); second and third grades, 2 mm (width of leading, 4.0 mm); fourth grade, 1.8 mm (width of leading, 3.6 mm). "The vertical strokes of letters should be thick enough to stand out clearly and distinctly." Concerning those factors on which no objective data were available, it was proposed that the recommendations of expert printers should be followed.

The need of additional research was emphasized in connection with every factor studied. In order to determine, for example, the effect of style of type on legibility, all other characteristics of printed material should be held constant more rigorously than had been true in earlier studies. Furthermore, the need for the development and use of accurate methods of measuring eye strain or fatigue in reading was recognized clearly. "Because of the large number of eye defects among school children, it is very important that debatable issues be studied in detail with respect to both normal and abnormal vision."

Recent Developments

During the last decade investigations have centered largely on seven issues. The first relates to the surface and color of the paper. Taylor (12: No. 90), Holmes (8: No. 55), and Paterson and Tinker (8: No. 80) secured evidence supporting earlier findings to the effect that black print on white background is more legible than any other combination involved in their experiments including white print on a black background.

Concerning the surface and tint of the paper, Stanton and Burtt (13: No. 72) found that they did not influence speed of reading appreciably. Webster and Tinker (12: No. 104), experimenting with eggshell, artisan enamel, and flint enamel paper stock, failed to find any "differential effect" during short reading periods. They concluded that the alleged eye strain resulting from reading print on glazed paper "must be due entirely to continuous reading in light not uniformly dispersed rather than to inability to see the print satisfactorily."

A second problem relates to length of line. Gates (8: No. 38) summarized available evidence in this field and concluded that further research is needed before final conclusions can be reached concerning the optimal length of line.

Size of type was studied with special reference to its effect on speed of reading. Buckingham (8: No. 6) reported data which showed that 12-point type ranked first, 14- and 18-point type ranked second, and 24-point type ranked third when read by first-grade children. Alderman (16: No. 2) presented materials printed in 8-, 10-, 12-, and 14-point type to pupils in grades 1 to 6 inclusive. He found that the smaller type was read more rapidly in both the upper and lower grades. This was true for pupils of different intelligence levels. On the basis of evidence secured through the Betts telebinoculars, he concluded that all who have eyes good enough to engage successfully in schoolwork in general read the smaller type more rapidly than the larger type. Unfortunately, the tests given were of short duration and failed to consider the factor of fatigue. Furthermore, the influence of size of type on accuracy of word recognition in the early stages of learning to read was not studied.

The legibility of different type faces was studied by several investigators. Webster and Tinker (12: No. 103) determined by the distance method the relative legibility of ten type faces and found that the American typewriter face was the most legible of those studied. These findings differ significantly from those of previous studies in which legibility was measured in terms of speed of reading. Greene (12: No. 43) compared the speed and accuracy of reading Ionic linotype and American typewritten material when 7-point and 10-point type were used. The records showed only slight differences, superiority varying with the type used. Tinker (8: No. 102) found that old-style numerals are somewhat more legible than modern-style numerals when printed in isolation and much more legible when printed in groups. Such findings, while suggestive, have only limited value. The whole problem of the legibility of different type faces should be attacked as a unit so that accurate comparison may be made.

Wide interest has been expressed in the relative legibility of different typographical arrangements. For example, Paterson and Tinker (10: No. 64) compared material in 10-point, 19-pica line length, Scotch Roman, set with 1-, 2-, and 4-point leading with material in 10-point type and a 19-pica line length, set solid. They found that the 1-point leading had no advantage over text set solid but that 2-point leading increased speed of reading by 7.5 per cent whereas 4-point leading increased it only 5 per cent. The investigators pointed out that the advantage of 2-point leading over both smaller and larger amounts of space between lines may hold only for "the particular size of type and length of line used."

In a study of the influence of form of type on the perception of words, Tinker (9: No. 104) found "that total word-form is more potent in the perception of words in lower case than in capitals."

Concerning the amount of light essential for effective and comfortable vision, Tinker (16: No. 109) concluded after reviewing all the evidence available that "the critical level for reading is between 3 and 4 foot-candles." To provide a margin of safety he recommended that no reading should be done with less than 5 foot-candles of light. In schoolrooms the minimum "should probably not be less than about 10 foot-candles"; in sight-saving classes "the brightness should probably be 20 to 25 foot-candles."

The studies reported during recent years have made significant contributions to our understanding of the hygiene of reading. In many respects, however, confidence in traditional standards have been shaken, as shown by the findings of Buckingham and of Alderman concerning the relation of size of type to speed of reading, particularly in the lower grades. As in 1925 the need is urgent for better controlled studies of the relative legibility of different typographical arrangements and for the development and use of techniques which determine the effect of different factors and arrangements on fatigue or discomfort in reading.

Concluding Statement

The foregoing summary provides convincing evidence of the value of carefully planned research in clarifying and enriching understanding of reading problems. The facts and issues revealed suggest numerous types of studies which may be carried on to advantage both in the classroom and in the laboratory. In planning a program of research for the future, attention should be directed more largely than in the past to the learner and to the factors that influence his interest in reading and his progress in learning to read. Furthermore, the findings should be interpreted more explicitly in terms of progressive thought concerning the function of education and in the light of all that is known concerning child growth and development. Thus conceived, research in reading may continue to make notable contributions in the future at all levels of formal and informal education.

Bibliography

Note: This bibliography includes two types of references: first, references to monographs and articles by the writer which include summaries and annotated bibliographies of approximately two thousand scientific studies of reading and, second, a limited number of additional references which are of unusual significance or which were not included in previous summaries.

Summaries by William S. Gray
　1. *Summary of Investigations Relating to Reading.* Supplementary Educational Monographs, No. 28. University of Chicago Press, 1925. 276 p.
　2. "Summary of Reading Investigations (July 1, 1924, to June 30, 1925)." *El Sch J* 26: 449-59, 507-18, 574-84, 662-73: 1926.
　3. "―――― (July 1, 1925, to June 30, 1926)." *El Sch J* 27: 456-66, 495-510: 1927.
　4. "―――― (July 1, 1926, to June 30, 1927)." *El Sch J* 28: 443-59, 496-510, 587-602: 1928.
　5. "―――― (July 1, 1927, to June 30, 1928)." *El Sch J* 29: 443-57, 496-509: 1929.

6. "——— (July 1, 1928, to June 30, 1929)." *El Sch J* 30: 450-66, 496-508: 1930.
7. "——— (July 1, 1929, to June 30, 1930)." *El Sch J* 31: 531-46, 592-606: 1931.
8. "——— (July 1, 1930, to June 30, 1931)." *El Sch J* 32: 447-63, 510-20, 587-94: 1932.
9. "——— (July 1, 1931, to June 30, 1932)." *J Ed Res* 26: 401-24: 1933.
10. "——— (July 1, 1932, to June 30, 1933)." *J Ed Res* 27: 564-91: 1934.
11. "——— (July 1, 1933, to June 30, 1934)." *J Ed Res* 28: 401-24: 1935.
12. "——— (July 1, 1934, to June 30, 1935)." *J Ed Res* 29: 407-32: 1936.
13. "——— (July 1, 1935, to June 30, 1936)." *J Ed Res* 30: 553-76: 1937.
14. "——— (July 1, 1936, to June 30, 1937)." *J Ed Res* 31: 401-34: 1938.
15. "——— (July 1, 1937, to June 30, 1938)." *J Ed Res* 32: 481-517: 1939.
16. "——— (July 1, 1938, to June 30, 1939)." *J Ed Res* 33: 481-523: 1940.
17. "Special Methods in the Elementary School: Reading." *R Ed Res* 1: 247-60: 1931.
18. "Psychology of the School Subjects: Reading." *R Ed Res* 1: 328-36: 1931.
19. "Special Methods on the High-School Level: Reading and Literature." *R Ed Res* 2: 29-34: 1932.
20. "Curriculum Investigations at the Elementary- and Secondary-School Levels: A. Reading." *R Ed Res* 4: 135-38: 1934.
21. "Special Methods and Psychology of the Elementary-School Subjects: Reading." *R Ed Res* 5: 54-69: 1935.
22. "Curriculum Investigations: F. Reading." *R Ed Res* 7: 139-42: 1937.
23. "Special Methods and Psychology of the Elementary School Subjects: Reading." *R Ed Res* 7: 493-507: 1937.

Supplementary References

24. American Council on Education, Committee on Materials of Instruction. *The Story of Writing*. Achievements of Civilization, No. 1. 1932. 64 p.
25. American Council on Education, Committee on Reading in General Education. *Reading in General Education*. 1940. 464 p.
26. Boss, Mabel E. "Reading, Then and Now." *Sch and Soc* 51: 62-64: 1940.
27. Cheney, O.H. *Economic Survey of the Book Industry, 1930-31*. New York: National Association of Book Publishers, 1931. 337 p.
28. Duffus, R.L. *Books: Their Place in a Democracy*. Houghton, 1930. 225 p.
29. Gray, W.S. "Reading." *Thirty-eighth Yearbook*, N.S.S.E., Part I. Public-Sch., 1939. p. 185-209.
30. Huey, E.B. *The Psychology and Pedagogy of Reading*. Macmillan, 1912. 469 p.
31. Lamport, H.B. *A History of the Teaching of Beginning Reading*. Doctor's thesis. University of Chicago, 1935. 516 p.
32. Leonard, J.P. "English Language, Reading, and Literature." *R Ed Res* 4: 449-61, 520-24: 1934.
33. N.S.S.E. *Report of the National Committee on Reading*. Twenty-fourth Yearbook, Part I. Public-Sch., 1925. 335 p.
34. N.S.S.E. *The Teaching of Reading: A Second Report*. Thirty-sixth Yearbook, Part I. Public-Sch., 1937. 442 p.

35. Richards, I.A. *Interpretation in Teaching.* Harcourt, 1938. 420 p.
36. Smith, Nila B. *American Reading Instruction.* Silver, 1934. 288 p.
37. Strang, Ruth. *Problems in the Improvement of Reading in High School and College.* Science Press, 1938. 390 p.
38. Vernon, Magdalen D. *Studies in the Psychology of Reading.* Reports of the Committee upon the Physiology of Vision, III. Privy Council, Medical Research Council, Special Report Series, No. 130. London: H. M. Stationery Office, 1929. 190 p.
39. Vernon, Magdalen D. *Visual Perception.* London: Cambridge University Press, 1937. 247 p.